CREW ABOARD A SUPERYACHT

C000253728

A GUIDE TO WORKING AFLOAT

Kim Davis

ADLARD COLES NAUTICAL
London

I dedicate this book to Jacqui and Heather,
my gorgeous little reasons for living ashore

Published 2004 by Adlard Coles Nautical
an imprint of A & C Black Publishers Ltd
37 Soho Square, London W1D 3QZ
www.adlardcoles.com

First published in the USA as *The Yachtie Bible* 2002
by The Professional Projects Company

First edition published in the UK
by Adlard Coles Nautical 2004

ISBN 0-7136-7094-0

A CIP catalogue record for this book is
available from the British Library.

A & C Black uses paper produced with elemental
chlorine-free pulp, harvested from managed sustainable forests.

Typeset in Palatino
Printed and bound in Great Britain

Note: While all reasonable care has been taken in the
publication of this book, the publisher takes no responsibility
for the use of the methods or products described in the book.

CONTENTS

6 chapters
Appendix 1-5

ACKNOWLEDGEMENTS

As I complete this new edition of my book I must first thank my mother, Pat Cole, who has herself joined the ranks of the 'yachties'. Just a few years ago she retired at the usual sort of age, sold her business and her horse farm and bought a sailing catamaran. Then with her crew, a cocker spaniel named Patrick, and a bob-tailed cat named Dudley, Mom set off on a three year sailing adventure. I am so proud of her for facing her fears and developing the skills she needed to captain her vessel single-handedly. I feel honoured that she would even consider trying this lifestyle. Imitation really is the sincerest form of flattery.

I must offer heartfelt thanks to a number of people around the world for their contributions of photos. They include: for the cover photo, Judi Tucker and her former captain Bruce Preston of the sailing yacht *No Logic*, a Swan 112; Captain Renee Brescia of ANS Designs and www.seaitallhere.com; Jessica Devereaux of the sailing yacht *Seljm*; Karen Bain and the owners of the sailing yacht *Taeoo*; Claudette Delanoeye of Frank Gordon Yacht Sales in Ft Lauderdale; George Warren at Sea Love Marina, Ponce Inlet, Florida; and Captain Chuck for assisting with winches and cleats.

Thank you to all the people who provided information for this book. In an effort to be as accurate as possible, particularly with regard to licensing requirements, I traded emails with and spoke to many people; all were very gracious and generous with their time. In particular I want to say thank you to Jane Cooke at Fred Dovaston in Mallorca, www.yachtcrew.com, who helped me update the crew salary tables, and to Leisl Thompson and Virginia Murphy, and all the other 'yachtie.net crew' for keeping me updated about the state of the industry from the inside.

Thank you Quink for your boundless energy, enthusiasm and encouragement. I would not be here without you.

And thank you especially to my tall, funny English husband for encouraging me to pursue my passions. He really is my best friend.

About the author

Thanks to the documentary films of Jacques Cousteau, Kim Davis grew up feeling drawn to the sea. She studied marine biology at university but discovered that what she craved was adventure, not science. While doing research in the Florida Keys, Kim took a job in a scuba shop, and thus began her career with tourists on boats. She soon found herself in Ft Lauderdale, looking for work. Within two weeks she was crewing on a sport fishing boat, and within a few months she was working aboard a 98-foot motor yacht. That was 1980. In 1991, she married a handsome Englishman, and gave up sailing in 1994 when their first daughter was born. Today Kim, her Englishman, and their two beautiful little girls live in a small town in Texas.

The author on deck.

INTRODUCTION

This book is for would-be adventurers who dream of seeing the world. While international travel is easier today than it has ever been, it still requires time and money and most of us simply don't have enough of either. Sure, many gap year students take back-packing trips, but that type of travel isn't for everyone. What happens if you contract a deadly intestinal parasite in the Middle East, or run short of money in Timbuktu? Being sick or skint in a foreign country can be a frightening and dangerous experience.

The message here is that you very definitely can travel around the world for extended periods of time while earning a good living working aboard private yachts. This material has been compiled to assist those already working in the yachting industry as well as those just starting out. You will find detailed contact lists of crew placement agencies and training establish-ments around the world in the second half of the book, as well as a glossary of terms and a few charts and diagrams so you'll be able to 'speak the lingo' if you've never done this before.

Crewing for a living, even for just a few years, offers many advantages. Here are some of the reasons you might consider entering this exciting field: 217

- You don't need a university degree to get started.
- You don't have to join any clubs or organisations.
- You have the chance to see the world.
- You will meet some of the wealthiest and most famous people in the world.
- You will develop invaluable social skills.
- You will develop countless practical skills.
- Even entry-level salaries allow crew to build savings in the region of £11,000 ($20,000 US) annually.
- Charter yacht crews earn fantastic tips in addition to their salary.
- There are no overheads. While you are employed aboard a yacht you will have no rent or bills, and uniforms and meals will be provided.
- Your earnings will be largely tax-free.
- Most yachts give four weeks paid holiday, and while this may sound normal to many people, Americans are quite fortunate if they are granted two weeks paid holiday per year.
- Not a lot of people know about this industry, therefore there are never enough good people to fill the available positions.
- The trend among cruising yachts today is toward larger and more luxurious boats, therefore more crew positions are opening up all the time as brand new superyachts leave the builders' yards.

Don't worry about whether or not you have enough experience to do the job. You can learn most of the skills you need as you go, and this book will show you how to get the training you need to secure your first position. After that, if you enjoy yourself, and prove your ability to work well at close quarters with others, you will almost certainly progress rapidly up the pay scale.

Before you say, 'I couldn't do that, I get seasick', you need to know that everybody gets seasick. Later, we'll look at remedies you can use until you get your 'sea legs'. The important thing is to start working, which means:

- Getting to a place where there are superyachts.
- Getting to know other people working on the yachts once you get there.
- Convincing those other people that you are willing to work, and to learn.
- Satisfying minimum sea safety requirements by taking STCW – 95 Basic Safety Training. (We'll cover the what, where and how of this shortly.)

You could strike out without a clue like I did. I made plenty of mistakes, but I learned fast, and I was always willing to work. I owe my successes in the yachting industry to the many wonderful people who shared their knowledge along the way. Some were co-workers, some were employers, and some were just friends. The professional yachting community is very tight-knit, and you will never feel lonely once you join its ranks.

I wrote this book because I want to pass on some of the advice and assistance I had when I started. I also want to introduce others to the big wide world and its wonderful people and places. Let me be your guide for just a little while as you set out on this rewarding path. Crewing as a paid professional can be a brilliant way to see the world, make new friends, and lay a firm financial foundation for your future. I hope that it will bring you at least a little of the joy it has brought me.

Kim Davis
2004

A BRIEF OVERVIEW

What does being a yacht professional involve?

Firstly, how should we define the term 'yacht'? There are motor yachts and sailing yachts, and within the sailing yacht category there are cruising yachts and racing yachts. The sport of yacht racing, however popular, is huge and there is not enough room to do it justice here. This book focuses instead on how to find a job aboard a motor yacht or a sailing yacht designed for cruising.

There are thousands of yachts around the world. Cruising yachts are generally owned by individuals, but there are also some companies that own yachts for charter. Yachts with permanent crew range in size from about 20 metres to 200+ metres, and employ between two and 200 crewmembers.

Some yachts are strictly private, and some are used for charter. Private yachts are used by their owners and invited guests, while charter yachts are chartered or 'hired' out to paying guests by the week. Many yachts do a combination of both, with the owner using the boat for a portion of each season, and renting it out for the remainder. This is a good arrangement for owners, since it helps to offset the outrageous costs associated with maintaining a yacht.

The salaries on private yachts are a little higher and the work schedule tends to be slightly more relaxed. However, on charter yachts, which command between about £8,500 and £60,000 (and upwards for larger yachts) per week to rent, the crew receives a gratuity or tip at the end of the charter, which is generally 10-15% of the cost of the charter. Most crews split the tip evenly, so it is not unreasonable to expect to earn an extra £500–£1,000 per charter, tax-free. A busy charter vessel may do 20 or more charters per year, which means the crew are very busy, but the potential earnings compensate them well.

The average superyacht carries eight crew. These are: captain, first mate, engineer, chef, chief steward/stewardess, second steward/stewardess, and two deckhands. However, there are many smaller yachts that operate with only a captain, a chef and sometimes a deckhand.

Captains, first mates, and *engineers* must be licensed. They have to work for several years documenting the sea miles they travel before taking the courses required to obtain these certifications. In the UK the Maritime and Coastguard Agency (MCA) offers widely accepted certificates. In the United States, the US Coast Guard (USCG) is the licensing body, and in Australia the Australian Maritime Safety Agency (AMSA) issues the permits. For a full listing of all the world's maritime regulatory and licensing bodies visit www.ShipManager.info.

We will go into specific licensing requirements in the next chapter. The best thing you can do when you first start out is to keep a log of every sea mile you travel, and get your captain to sign off on it before you leave the employment of any vessel, however humble that vessel may be. Further information about licensing requirements may be obtained by going online to www.freedomyachting.com/Manning.htm.

The *chef* on a yacht is increasingly a trained position, though no license is officially required apart from the basic safety training that is now required for all paid crewmembers. The norm within the industry is for the chef to have some formal culinary training, and/or extensive work experience with written references. These references will be checked, so it doesn't pay to exaggerate your experience. The people you will be working for are accustomed to dining in the finest restaurants and hotels in the world. So if you can't put together a four-course meal for 25 on two hours' notice, by yourself, then you should probably do some training before applying for a yacht chef's position. I don't recommend starting a yachting career as chef because the hours are very long, and the galleys are small. In addition, while a restaurant kitchen's staff usually consists of an executive chef, sous chef, saucier, pastry chef, and various commis chefs, aboard a yacht the chef works alone with the exception of help plating the meals when a steward is available. So the average yacht chef must be well rounded and able to do all the cooking from breads and desserts to main courses and sauces. There is a brilliant online service, www.starchefs.com, that lists chef's training facilities all around the world if this sounds like the path you wish to follow.

Steward/stewardesses and *deckhands* need not have previous experience. These are the positions you will probably be applying for when you start out. Either of these positions is ideal for people between the ages of about 18 to 35, who are unencumbered by family commitments. All your expenses are paid, so you can save £11,000 ($20,000 US) per year, if you are sensible. You can also live like royalty and spend it all. The choice is yours.

Stewards and stewardesses are the housekeepers, the hosts and hostesses, the waiters and waitresses aboard yachts. Training is not currently required, but as the industry grows ever more professional, schools are starting up especially for yacht crew training, and they often offer training specifically for stewards. Here are several websites that advertise this type of class:

- www.uksa.org/ytcst2.html
- www.clubsail.com.au/yachtmaster_stewardess_courses_sailing_school.html
- www.crewbydrwoods.com
- www.americanyachtinstitute.com
- www.crewpacific.com.au

The entry level starting salary for steward/stewardesses is usually between £13,000 and £15,500 ($24,000 and $28,000 US) per year.

Deckhands keep the outside of the yacht clean and tidy, and assist with the helm and line handling while underway and docking. On smaller yachts, they may be expected to do some steward duties as well. Deckies will earn between £12,000 and £16,500, ($21,600 and $30,000 US) per year.

How do you get started as a yacht professional?

First of all, get your passport updated. Do a little research to find out which countries you need visas to visit. You can obtain visas for countries you think you will be visiting in advance. This will make life easier for you and your captain later on. When a job is offered, you will probably be expected to join the crew immediately, and there may not be enough time for long visits to the consulate.

Then you need a CV/résumé and letters of reference. Include a good head and shoulders photograph of yourself.

Finally, you have to go to a place where big yachts congregate. You need enough money for a round-trip airfare to get there (and back again) plus food, rent and transportation money enough for the first month. These costs will vary widely depending on where you decide to go in search of a job. The minimum amount of cash you'll need to cover your first month's expenses is £600, or $1000 US, but this sum could be considerably higher in some upmarket ports. In Chapter 3 you will find details about which ports are best suited to this sort of job hunt as well as a short list of crew houses and hostels in the world's top yachting cities. Plan to spend an additional £600, or $1000 US for basic safety training. You'll make this money back in your first month on a boat. In fact, if you go to a busy yachting port like Antibes, France; Palma de Mallorca, Spain; or Ft Lauderdale, Florida, you can even earn most of your expense money by doing day work while training and looking for permanent work.

You should have the senior officer on every boat you work on write a letter like the following sample certificate of MCA Watchkeeping Service and Testimonial (see page 6). It should be typed onto company/vessel stationery. If you apply for a license later, this documentation process will save a lot of headaches, since you will already have your cruising experience documented, and it can be next to impossible to locate former skippers to get them to sign off on your sea time after the fact. This format should satisfy most countries' requirements (for worldwide links to country specific info, visit www.shipmanager.info).

Good places to look for work

Spring and autumn are the best times to look for jobs aboard yachts as skippers are getting their crews together for the upcoming charter season. (Detailed information about placement agencies is given later in the book.)

Southampton, England

This is a great place to train. There are numerous sailing schools in the area that operate year round, but having done a Yachtmaster course there in late December, I recommend that you do practical sailing courses in warmer months. I nearly broke my neck sliding across icy pontoons in wellington boots!

(Date)

UK Maritime and Coastguard Agency
Bay 2/1, Spring Place
105 Commercial Road
Southampton SO15 1EG
UK
RE: Sea Service and Testimonial for (crew member name)

Dear Sir or Madam:

This letter is to certify that:
    (Full name of crewmember, First, Middle, and Last)
    (Crewmember's date of birth)
    (Discharge book No or passport number)

Has served on:
(Name of vessel)   (Official number)   (Type of vessel)
(Type of main propelling machinery)   (Gross tonnage)
(Area of operation)   From (date)   To (date)

in the capacity of (1st, 2nd, 3rd, 4th) Watchkeeping Officer under my command. During this period the above named crewmember had full charge of a (deck, engine) watch for not less than (number) hours out of every 24 hours whilst the vessel was on (unlimited, near coastal) voyages.

In addition, the above named crewmember: (include the following as appropriate)
1. Regularly carried out other duties in connection with routine and maintenance of the ship.
2. Served as the (senior, junior) of two watchkeeping officers during the following periods when (bridge/engine room) watches were doubled, and at no other times, as follows:
    _____
3. Was granted no leave of absence; or was granted leave of absence as follows: _____ which period(s) (was, were) deducted from (his, her) total leave entitlement.
4 Served on board the vessel from (date) to (date) whilst it was in the final stages of construction.

My report on the service of the above named officer during the period stated is as follows:
Conduct: (remarks), Experience/Ability: (remarks), Behaviour: (remarks)

Sincerely,
(Signature of Master/Chief Engineer/Owner/Authorized Official)
(Typed name of above signatory and position)
(Company stamp and date)

Palma de Mallorca, Spain

This place is home to several famous yacht harbours and shipyards which cater specifically to superyachts. There are several busy yacht brokers and placement agencies to assist with finding a job, as well as affordable youth hostels for temporary accommodation. As with the other starting points, spring and summer are the best times to be looking for work here, though there is day work and maintenance work available year round. If you are travelling from the UK or Germany look into package holiday rates since it is often less expensive to fly this way than to book a regular ticket. You don't need to speak Spanish here, since just about everyone in the yachting business speaks English.

Antibes, France

Antibes is the 'Fort Lauderdale of the Mediterranean'. There is a great deal of work to be found here, and excellent services geared specifically to yacht crew, including abundant placement agencies, training facilities, and temporary accommodation. Spring and summer are the best times to arrive here, but there is work year-round. Don't worry if your French is a bit rusty. English is spoken here.

New Zealand

Summer here is from November to March. This is a favourite place to spend the cyclone season in the South Pacific. The main yachting centres are on the North Island in Auckland, Whangarei and the Bay of Islands. The Kiwis take yachting very seriously, with many prestigious yacht races sponsored there. There are some crew placement agencies in Auckland, but this branch of the yachting industry is not as well established as the racing tradition. New Zealand is gaining a reputation for building fine yachts, and if you originate in this part of the world, it would be worthwhile pursuing the yachting industry through the boatbuilders. With new boats being launched regularly, there is always the need for crew.

Australia

Australia, like New Zealand, is more often associated with yacht racing than yacht chartering. However, there are some crew placement agencies listed in Appendix 4, and many sailing schools.

Ft Lauderdale, Florida

Ft Lauderdale is the most crewmember friendly place in the world, and spring and autumn are the best times to be there. There are abundant resources for new and experienced crew alike. The crew placement agencies in Ft Lauderdale work with yachts around the world, so starting here can save a lot of time and aggravation. The mild climate all year round makes this a yacht haven, and crew of every nationality routinely find work here.

Newport, Rhode Island

This is a very popular summer yacht spot. There are quite a few agencies and services here, but unless you get a job with a boat-builder you won't find much work in the freezing winter months.

English Harbour, Antigua

Antigua has it all going on in the spring and autumn, and it is particularly famous for 'Race Week' in April. Nelson's Dockyard also plays host to 'Agents Week' in November. Chances are, as a crewmember you will make it to Antigua at some point, and once you've gotten through customs there, it is a great place to look for a job. The hitch is that when you enter the country, you must have a valid plane ticket home or you must be signed on as permanent crew aboard a yacht already. Many a crewmember has been deported from Antigua for not having their departure plans in place when they arrive. We had particular trouble in Antigua after an Atlantic crossing when we arrived with a South African delivery crew aboard, who had planned to look for work, or travel once they left us. The Antiguan customs officials insisted that we provide air fare to South Africa for these individuals. In the end other less costly arrangements were made, but it was a hassle none of us needed at the time.

Delivery positions

The following ports are interesting and exotic places to look for non-paying delivery positions, but beware! Unscrupulous people really do exist, and past yacht hitchhikers have been known to find themselves in compromising situations. A few have even disappeared never to be seen again. Deliveries are usually long trips, and once you leave the dock it could be weeks before you see land again. Look carefully at the boat and everyone else who will be sailing with it before you accept a position. Here are a few questions you must ask before setting sail:

- Is there a recently inspected liferaft?
- How new is the radio?
- Is the captain licensed?
- Is he/she sober?
- Does he have the course plotted for the next port of call?
- Does he know how to plot the course for the next port of call?
- Is there enough food?
- Are there any hidden costs to you?
- Has anyone aboard made unwanted sexual advances or comments?

If anything about a prospective boat, its skipper or crew makes you uncomfortable, give it a miss. Another boat will come along. Better safe than dead or worse…

Regarding drugs on yachts: **don't let yourself be found anywhere near any illegal substance on a boat!** You will be considered guilty by association if you are travelling on a boat used for drug smuggling. For that matter, watch out for 'people smuggling' as well.

Even if you are not getting paid, don't forget to have the skipper sign a letter listing the sea miles you travelled, what your job was while on board, where you started and where you finished. Also ask for a separate written reference. You'll need at least a couple of these when applying for paid positions.

Gibraltar

If you get here in October/November, you will find many boats heading from the Mediterranean to the Caribbean. In the spring, they're returning, but as they're nearly home, there are not as many jobs then. Nearly all yachts entering and leaving the Mediterranean stop here because the fuel is cheap. The most reasonable accommodations are in Algeciras, a Spanish town across the footbridge. Fly to Madrid and take a train to Gibraltar from there.

Panama

Be there March/April. Hotels, food and flights are all reasonably priced. Boats congregate in two areas; one on either side of the canal. Offer to help folks cross the canal. This will give you a chance to assess the boats and the people on board before committing to a longer trip.

Mexico

Cabo San Lucas and Puerto Vallarta. February/March is the time to find boats from California looking for delivery crew. Flights are cheap if you can get on a charter, and the food is very reasonably priced.

Thailand

Phuket. Be there in January.

Galle Harbour, Sri Lanka

Be there February/March. Both Thailand and Sri Lanka cost next to nothing once you're there. Check for travellers' advisories before visiting this often-troubled region. You must also keep in mind that piracy still exists with Indonesia, Bangladesh, and Nigeria topping the list of most frequent pirate attacks reported in 2003. Know what you are getting into before you set out for these beautiful ports. Online, you can check www.dockwalk.com for the latest piracy report, which is compiled annually by:

The IMB Piracy Reporting Centre
Kuala Lumpur, Malaysia
Tel: +60 3 2031 0014
Fax: +60 3 2078 5769
24 Hours Anti Piracy helpline tel: +60 3 2031 0014

2

CREW RESPONSIBILITIES
AND QUALIFICATIONS

Licenses and Training

Until 1995 the international maritime training requirements concerned mainly crews on tankers. This meant that with the exception of the captain, the first mate and the engineer, crewmembers aboard passenger-carrying ships, ferries, or yachts were not required to be licensed or trained. This is pretty scary since the training in question is largely involved with life saving, survival at sea and pollution control in the event of a disaster. As of June 1 2002 however, this changed. Consequently, it is no longer quite as simple to get a job on a yacht, but the seas are safer for everyone, including the crews.

The International Maritime Organization (IMO), a specialized United Nations agency, is the international governing body responsible for maritime safety and for preventing pollution from ships. In 1978 they first drafted the Standards of Training, Certification and Watchkeeping (STCW), which was aimed primarily at tanker crews. Then in 1995, prompted by the September '94 disaster when the ferry *Estonia* sank as it crossed the Baltic taking an estimated 852 lives, these guidelines were revised resulting in the STCW – 95.

It has taken a while for the 157 IMO member nations to implement and set up regulatory bodies to police STCW – 95 compliance, and there are still less developed countries in particular, that are not in compliance. July 1 2004 sees major policing policy changes taking place in the US which will require all foreign registered vessels entering the country to be boarded by the Coastguard to assure that they are in compliance with the STCW and that there are no terrorists on board.

American captains, mates and engineers are also finding new tougher licensing regulations coming into force (see www.dock-walk.com/issues/2004/march/ask_amy2.shtml). In Australia, following a decision by the Australian Maritime Safety Agency (AMSA) not to recognize UK STCW – 95 ancillary training courses/certificates, the MCA has chosen not to recognize several AMSA advanced STCW certificates. The MCA will continue to recognize the 4-element basic STCW training that affects readers of this book. (For more detailed information about licensing requirements for yacht crews, see www.freedomyachting.com.)

'Alright,' you ask, 'how does all of this affect me?'

Basically, as a paid crewmember on a yacht you will be considered professional crew and you will have to do some basic safety training. Furthermore, insurance companies are demanding that yacht crew be totally compliant with the Basic Safety Training even in cases where the law does not. If you can't afford to pay for the course you can still begin sending your CV to placement agencies, with the understanding that your STCW Basic Safety Training is pending. You may be able to land an entry-level position without it, provided you spend your first paycheck on the 5-day STCW Compliant Basic Safety Course. If you are in a yachting centre, you will be able to do some daywork while completing this basic training program. The course will take 1 week, and costs will vary depending on where you take it.

STCW – 95 Basic Safety Training
- 2 days basic firefighting
- 1 day First Aid
- $1^1/2$ days Sea Survival Training
- $1/2$ day Personal Safety and Social Responsibility.

Here is a partial listing of organizations where you can inquire about training (also see Appendix 5):

Hoylake Sailing School in association with John Percival Marine Associates (JPMA)

Offers many courses tailored to suit the superyacht industry. In addition, JMPA work closely with a number of UK marine training establishments so they are able to organize training plans for individuals to suit their work/leave schedules.

John Percival Marine Associates (JPMA)
Tel: +44 (0) 151 632 4000
Fax: +44 (0) 151 632 4776
Email: captain@hss.ac.uk
Web: www.hss.ac.uk/MCACourses.html

South Tyneside College – Marine Safety Training Centre (UK)

The STCW Basic Safety Training info may not be online, so it's best to call or e-mail for details.

Marine Safety Training Centre
South Tyneside College
Wapping Street
South Shields
Tyne & Wear
NE33 1LQ
Tel: +44(0) 191 427 3642
Fax: +44(0) 191 427 3600
Email: marineshortcourse@stc.ac.uk
Web: www.stc.ac.uk
MCA approved, cost: £760 for UK residents, and £935 for non-UK residents.

United Kingdom Sailing Academy (UK)

This school offers a unique selection of courses designed specifically for the yachting industry.

UKSA
West Cowes
Isle of Wight
PO31 7PQ
Tel: +44 (0) 1983 294941
Fax: +44 (0) 1983 295938
Email: info@uksa.org
Web: www.uksa.org

Blue Water Yachting

Offering courses in Antibes, France; Palma de Mallorca, Spain; and Viareggio, Italy.

Blue Water Yachting
La Galarie du Port
8 Blvd d'Aguillon
06600 Antibes,
France
Tel: +33 (0) 4 93 34 34 13
Fax: +33 (0) 4 93 34 35 93
Web: www.bluewater-
  charter.com/training/
  courses.php
MCA approved, cost: €1200

M & O Group of Companies

Australian home office with regional offices around the world.

Web: www.mando.com.au/
  training_courses.htm

For training information contact:
President/CEO Mr Rick Parish –
  rick.parish@mando.biz
Group General Manager
Mr Andrew Maffett –
  Andrew.maffett@mando.biz

Or contact the appropriate regional office:
Angola – james.smith@
  sonangol.co.ao
Australia –
  judyth.lyon@mando.biz
GCC Countries (excluding
  Qatar) – mando@dma-
  consulting.com.sa
Kazakhstan – director@YKK.kz
Middle East (including Qatar) –
  tasha@qatar.net.qa
New Zealand –
  darryn.chelley@mando.biz
South Africa –
  dupresq@mweb.do.zq
Venezuela –
  Fernando@montuenga.com

Fisheries and Marine Institute of Memorial University of Newfoundland - Offshore Safety and Survival Center (Canada)

PO Box 4920

St John's

Newfoundland

A1C 5R3

Canada

Tel: +1 (709) 834 2076 or

toll-free: (800) 563 5799

Fax: +1 (709) 834 1344

Email: ossc@mi.mun.ca

MCA approved; call for pricing.

Sea Horse Academy of Merchant Navy (India)

#7-9-40 Sambamurthy Street

Ramaraopet

Kakinada – 533.004

India

Tel: +91 884 2371220

Mobile: 09848 172669

Fax: +91 884 2342843

Email: shamn@vsnl.com or

rmy_seahorse@sancharnet.in

Web:

www.seahorseacademy.com

Mahurangi Technical Institute (New Zealand)

11 Glenmore Drive

PO Box 414

Warkworth

New Zealand

Tel: +64 (0) 9 425 8493

Freephone: 0800 DONT SINK

Fax: +64 (0) 9 425 8928

Email: info@mti.net.nz

Web:

www.mahurangitech.co.nz

MCA approved, cost: $1091 NZ

Chapman School of Seamanship (USA)

4343 SE St Lucie Blvd

Stuart

FL 34997

USA

Tel: (800) 225 2841, or +1 (772) 283 8130

Fax: +1 (772) 283 2019

Email: info@chapman.org

Web: www.chapman.org

USCG Approved, cost: $795

Maritime Professional Training (USA)

1915 South Andrews Avenue
Ft Lauderdale
FL 33316
USA
Tel: (888) 839 5025, or
+1 (954) 525 1014
Email: info@mptusa.com
Web: www.mptusa.com
USCG approved, cost: $895 US

Maritime Science Department – Clatsopcollege (USA)

6550 Liberty Lane
Astoria
Oregon 97103
USA
Tel: +1 (503) 325 7962 or
+1 (503) 338 7600
Email: msd-info@clatsopcc.edu
Web: www.clatsopcollege.com/
maritime/stcw.html
USCG and MCA approved,
cost: $650 US

Resolve Fire and Hazard Response Inc (USA)

PO Box 165485
Port Everglades
Florida 33316, USA
Tel: +1 (954) 463 9195
Toll Free: (888) 886 FIRE
Fax: +1 (954) 356 5898
Web: www.resolvefire.com
USCG and MCA approved,
cost: $895 US

Sea Schools (USA)

Tel: (800) 237 8663
Web:
www.seaschool.com/STCW.htm
STCW courses offered in
Jacksonville, Florida, and in
Bayou La Batre, Alabama.
USCG approved, cost: $495 US
in Jacksonville, or $595 US in
Bayou La Batre (the extra $100
covers the cost of room and
board.)

Captain's responsibilities

★ First and foremost, the yacht captain must ensure the safety of every person on board, whether they are owners, guests or crew. His word is law aboard the vessel, and as such he or she is the person held accountable in the event of any accident involving the yacht or its tenders.

*A good captain acts as a mentor for junior crewmembers,
providing opportunities for them to hone their skills.*

★ He must be familiar with all licensing required by the IMO, MCA, and USCG for the crew and the vessel.

★ He is ultimately responsible for establishing safety procedures on board, including drills and equipment to be used. He may delegate this task to the first mate and engineer.

★ He creates crew job descriptions. The basic jobs are the same wherever you go, but each vessel will have unique requirements, and the captain decides who is responsible for each chore.

★ He sets an example and establishes guidelines regarding crew appearance and behaviour both on board and ashore. A really good captain acts as a mentor for junior crewmembers, providing opportunities for them to hone their skills. He should inspire respect in his crew.

    • He makes sure that the crew understands how to interact properly with owners and guests. (Different yachts cater to different sorts of people, but it is safe to assume that the crew should be friendly without being overly familiar with the guests.)

- In addition, he sets guidelines for crew etiquette ashore. (Drunk and disorderly behaviour ashore is frowned upon, since it reflects badly on the yacht.)

★ He deals with guests and contract labourers, maintaining a professional demeanour at all times. For example, if a captain feels that too much is being asked of his crew by owners or guests, it is his responsibility to make this clear to the parties making the unreasonable requests.

★ He must be able to safely manoeuvre the vessel, and he must be a competent and proficient navigator.

★ He must have a thorough working knowledge of all mechanical and electronic equipment onboard.

★ He must have a complete knowledge of customs and immigration procedures and documentation for the vessel and crew. There will be times when research is called for. For example, it is extremely helpful if the captain knows ahead of time in which countries the customs officials expect a bribe, and how to discreetly provide one, whether it is in the form of whisky, cigarettes or US dollars.

★ He must have a thorough knowledge of employment and charter laws.

★ He must create and maintain an operating budget for the yacht. He is responsible for all the yacht's accounting, and for all inventory control on board, though the other officers oversee their own inventories.

★ He plans and manages major refits as well as routine repairs and maintenance. This includes undertaking all negotiations and dispute resolution with yard personnel regarding price and quality of service.

★ He must keep abreast of changes and developments in international qualification standards.

★ He must organize the yacht's itinerary, including making all dockage reservations.

Captains qualifications

He must be licensed appropriately based on the vessel's tonnage, the waters cruised and the insurance required, including satisfying all STCW compliance requirements.

He must have extensive maritime experience, preferably with at least a few years on yachts. Even with years at sea, if a captain is not known within the industry, no one will hire him for a position as captain. He may have to build references as a first mate in order to be recognized as trustworthy within the yachting industry.

He must be able to remain calm in stressful situations, since he will face fantastic challenges of every sort on a daily basis. A well-developed sense of humour is a big plus!

First mate's responsibilities

★ Though he may never have to do so, the first mate must be fully capable of assuming control of the yacht and performing all of the captain's duties should the captain be unable to perform them himself for any reason.

★ Otherwise, the main responsibility of the first mate is to supervise and train the deck crew, including any junior officers.

★ He must ensure the safe handling of all operational and recreational deck equipment by crew and guests.

★ He often plans and implements safety procedures for both crew and guests including drills and training on equipment to be used. In addition he makes sure that all onboard safety equipment is maintained in good working order.

★ He ensures that all crew have received the required training and certificates for their positions.

★ He trains and supervises the deck crew in the use of all maintenance equipment and products, as well as doing a share of the work (ie painting, varnishing, cleaning and polishing).

The first mate must be proficient in all areas of deck maintenance.

★ He oversees docking and anchoring procedures, ensuring safe anchor, fender and line handling by the crew.
★ He updates charts and software.
★ He must be a proficient navigator and radio operator.
★ He creates watch lists and drills for the crew.
★ He provisions and maintains an inventory of deck supplies.
★ He has an understanding of all environmental pollution regulations as they pertain to the vessel in any given location.
★ He must understand and ensure that all maritime flag, anchor, navigation lights and tender protocols are followed.
★ He supervises all work areas throughout the boat making certain that they are presentable regardless of the work being carried out.
★ He maintains a professional demeanour in all situations.
★ He should have an overall knowledge of customs requirements for both ship and crew.

First mate's qualifications

Licensing as required by vessel tonnage and waters cruised. Previous yachting experience on vessels of comparable size or larger.

Positive, hard-working attitude. He should be a crew motivator, as opposed to being an oppressor.

STCW – 95 compliance including: Advanced First Aid, CPR, and Automated Defibrillator usage.

Engineer's responsibilities

Of special note with regard to the engineer's position is the fact that there is a huge demand right now for licensed engineers. Therefore, licensed engineers are commanding high salaries. If you have mechanical talent, this may be something to consider.

★ The engineer must have a thorough understanding of all machinery and systems on board including:

- Electrical systems
- Refrigeration
- Plumbing and sanitation systems, including various pumps and marine toilets
- Hydraulic systems
- Diesel mechanics, including main engines and generators
- Tenders and toys, including jet ski, wave runner etc
- Watermakers
- Electronics, including radio, radar, GPS etc
- Interior and exterior hardware repair, including winches and anchor windlass

★ The engineer creates and implements a preventative maintenance program for all mechanical equipment on board which includes maintaining inspection logs, scheduled maintenance logs, and engine room watch logs.

Talented engineers are always in demand.

★ He monitors and logs fuel and water usage, and tells the captain and/or first officer when it is time to refuel and take on water.

★ He implements safety procedures and preventive measures for the engineering department, fuelling, and transfers of pollutants.

★ The engineer conducts crew safety training on every aspect of the engineering department. Each crewmember should be familiar and comfortable with the engine room, mechanical and electrical safety and watchkeeping responsibilities underway and within the engine room.

★ He keeps an accurate and complete inventory of parts.

★ He should keep his work area and himself presentable at all times regardless of the work in progress, whether ashore or on board. This can prove a huge challenge for most engineers!

★ He will have to interact with guests and contract labourers, and maintain a professional attitude at all times.

★ He understands all onboard electronic navigational equipment, both how to maintain it and how to use it.

★ He has good navigational skills, including knowledge of rules of the road.
★ He must adhere to environmental catastrophe management regulations as required by law, in the case of oil spills, bilge pumping, waste disposal etc.
★ Above all, he must have a special talent for troubleshooting.

Engineer's qualifications

Must be licensed as required by vessel tonnage, waters cruised, and machinery onboard.

Must have previous maritime and mechanical experience, with some having been on yachts if possible, but this is not absolutely necessary.

Must have a positive, hardworking attitude and be willing to work long hours if necessary without complaint.

Must meet STCW – 95 compliance requirements, preferably with advanced firefighting training.

Deckhand's responsibilities

★ The deckhand is in charge of the upkeep of the yacht's exterior under the supervision of the first mate. If there is no first mate, the deckhand answers directly to the captain.
★ He/she assists the engineer with the maintenance of all deck equipment.
★ He/she carries out watches both underway and as designated duty person (since someone must remain onboard at all times, a watch rotation is usually followed).
★ He/she must follow safe operating procedures when anchoring, docking, refuelling, disposing of waste etc. The deckhand handles lines and fenders while docking.
★ The deckhand implements maritime flag, anchor, navigation

Deckies don't go ashore until all the salt spray is washed away.

lights and tender protocols under the supervision of the first mate, or captain.

★ Deckhands assist the owner and guests with luggage, water toys, shore excursions, and miscellaneous other services as requested. Deckies should be friendly and willing to help without being overly familiar.

★ Deckhands maintain work areas in a presentable state regardless of activity.

★ He/she presents a professional attitude and appearance at all times.

★ On smaller yachts, the deckhand may share engineer's duties with the captain and steward's duties with the chef.

Deckhand's qualifications

STCW – 95 Basic Safety Training.

Previous experience with any sort of boating or water

sports is a plus, including waterskiing, windsurfing, dinghy sailing, and scuba diving. Always include any certifications and club memberships in these areas.

Since the deck crew spend a great deal of time painting and varnishing, some experience with a paintbrush is very handy. Mechanical training or experience is useful.

Previous experience in any service industry is helpful, as the deckhand is sometimes required to assist with serving at tables and bartending.

As with all the other jobs on a boat, the deckhand must have a good attitude, and a willingness to 'get the job done'. Outgoing personalities do well, provided the privacy of others is respected. In other words, the deckie should know when to shut up.

Chef's responsibilities

★ The chef is well paid, but works the longest hours on the yacht. He/she is usually the first person up in the morning, and the last one to bed.

★ The chef is responsible for all food and drinks provisioning, and must maintain adequate supplies at all times. He/she is responsible for ensuring that all food and drink provisions are properly stored. (The chief steward sometimes assumes responsibility for maintaining wine and spirits stores.)

★ The chef must prepare and cook 2-3 nutritionally balanced meals per day for guests and crew. On some very large yachts, there may be a separate cook for the crew. The meals should be varied and interesting and chef should present even simple meals in an artistic and pleasing way.

★ He/she must use all perishable foods like meat and produce efficiently to minimise waste since storage space is limited, and it is not always convenient to go shopping.

★ Chef must plan all menus, but remain highly versatile and able to adjust the menu at a moment's notice, especially if a guest requests a change. Charter brokers will have supplied a food preference sheet detailing guests' food preferences and special needs, but often not all the guests are consulted when this sheet is filled out, so be prepared for surprises.

★ He/she must keep all food preparation and storage areas clean and sanitary at all times. On larger yachts there will be a steward to assist with this, but on smaller yachts, the chef may be responsible for the steward's duties as well. When cooking at sea, a special clean-as-you-go technique is required since unsecured pots and cookware tend to go flying.

★ The chef maintains accounting records for all galley purchases.

★ He/she keeps all galley equipment in good and sanitary working order.

The art is in the preparation of a good meal,
but also in the ability to cover up mistakes.

★ He/she assists with boat handling as necessary, including line and fender handling, and on smaller yachts, helming and watchkeeping.

★ The chef must maintain a clean, professional appearance at all times. Including hair either tied back or under a hat when cooking. Guests can't resist visiting the galley; especially right before meal times when they are hungry.

Chef's qualifications

STCW – 95 including Advanced Fire Fighting, CPR, and Advanced First Aid.

Previous experience aboard a vessel of comparable size or larger.

An ability to maintain a calm and pleasant demeanour while working long hours. The phrase 'no problem' should roll from his/her tongue regardless of the request. For example, in response to the request,'Can we do lunch for 10 in 20 minutes?'The cool chef replies,'No problem.' Chef then extracts the emergency side of salmon from the freezer, sends the deckie to the bakery, boils a dozen eggs, slices three tomatoes and an onion and opens a tin of caviar. (Caviar, expensive champagne and truffles always make the chef look good with very little effort expended!)

Increasingly, employers are looking for formal culinary training or apprenticeships. However, this is not strictly necessary. A good cook who can maintain a smile while working 14-hour days is assured of finding a job with or without formal training. With credentials from a culinary academy, however, the pay is higher. There is a good online listing of training establishments at www.starchefs.com.

Alternately, shore-based catering experience in hotels, restaurants, or as a domestic chef can satisfy reference requirements.

A chef should be a person who enjoys eating as well as cooking. Cooking is an art, and a good cook must be able to blend flavourings creating subtle differences in every meal. I once worked with a 'chef' who produced meals that looked wonderful, but because she never tasted her own cooking, everything tasted like cardboard. The ability to read a cookbook doesn't hurt either!

Steward/stewardess's responsibilities

★ The steward(ess) on a yacht is the hostess, housekeeper, waitress and bartender rolled into one. Larger yachts have a 'head stew', who acts in a supervisory capacity for the one to three junior stewards. The head stew is expected to take care of financial record keeping, performance evaluation, work scheduling, provisioning and inventory. He/she answers directly to the captain. Head stews earn quite respectable incomes, and this is a position to consider as you progress up the ladder of responsibility within the industry.

★ The stewards are responsible for keeping the yacht's interior clean and tidy at all times. There is a special art involved here, since the space is limited, and the cleaning chores must be carried out in the most unobtrusive way possible. For example, beds are made and heads (marine bathrooms) are usually cleaned while the guests are having breakfast. The vacuuming of the carpets is often done while the guests are ashore.

★ He/she is responsible for turning down the guests' beds at night. Once again, the prime opportunity to do this is while the guests are at dinner.

★ The steward serves all meals. Some meals are quite formal, and require formal table settings with china, silver and crystal. Silver service training may give job applicants an edge here.

★ When laying a formal table, the steward should know how to fold linen napkins in a variety of styles to complement the meal.

★ The steward should be creative and liaise with the chef when there is a 'theme' meal planned, in order to present the most interesting setting possible. The objective is to ensure that the guests have a pleasant and memorable stay onboard.

★ However impractical, yachts generally keep fresh flower arrangements on board. Therefore, the steward should know some basic flower arranging.

★ As host/hostess, the steward should take the initiative to gather tourist leaflets and other helpful information about the places the yacht will be visiting. These may be left for the guests in their cabins.

★ The stewards are responsible for all laundry. Many yachts have a washer and dryer, but when there is a lot of washing to be done, like when the bed linens have all been changed, the stew is responsible for getting the laundry to an outside service and ensuring that everything comes back from the laundry. This means that whenever the laundry leaves the boat, a detailed list must be made, and everything on the list must be checked when it returns. The name of the yacht should be somewhere on all sheets and towels.

★ As part of the laundry responsibilities, the steward/stewardess is expected to iron the table linens and often the bed linens as well. Besides making everything look nice, this practice helps avoid the natural tendency for mould to grow that exists on boats of all sizes. Guests will often have clothing that requires ironing as well.

★ The steward is also expected to help the chef with meal preparation and dishwashing.

Steward/stewardess's qualifications

STCW – 95 Basic Safety Training. Any additional lifesaving training or nursing experience is very helpful.

Valid driver's licence. An international driving licence is best, though not absolutely necessary.

Though some training establishments are springing up offering job specific training for yacht stewards, this training is not a requirement. It can't hurt, but previous experience in another service industry like hotels, restaurants, or catering can be even more useful if you can provide written references.

A clean, fresh appearance and a cheerful disposition are absolutely essential in this position.

Thomas S Wissmann at the International Yacht Sales Group wrote this regarding crew placement through their offices:

'All levels of experience are welcome. A number of our crews have been gaining more experience and we can offer them better jobs when they have improved. Nevertheless, we have a high standard of service and sometimes people fall through our net because they are not clean and tidy for a start.'

Crew Salaries

There are many factors involved in determining crew salaries. Supply and demand, the location of the boat, its itinerary and the time of year for a start. Whether or not the yacht will be chartering will also affect the pay. Traditionally, large yachts pay better than small ones, and charter yachts pay less than strictly private ones, but the potential for earning tips can compensate.

Other considerations include:

◆ Will all food costs be covered?
◆ Does the boat provide uniforms? Boat shoes?
◆ How much paid vacation time will there be?
◆ Will the boat pay for any additional training that may be required?

- What about health insurance? Most boats will be covered against accidental injury in the service of the boat, but if there is no regular health insurance coverage offered to the crew, buy it for yourself. Don't get sick or injured in a foreign port without it. Some of the better jobs aboard yachts today include full health benefits and pension schemes, but don't assume anything. Ask what is covered before you accept a job.
- What is the captain's reputation? Is he well liked or despised? A placement agent should be able to tell you this, or you may ask the captain for an opportunity to chat with the other crewmembers about the job.
- What is the yacht's reputation for crew turnover? A high paying job on a boat with high turnover is not as beneficial in the long run as a long-term happy job on a boat that pays a little less.
- A captain may ask for a probationary period when you start. Often this is because he does not expect you to work out, but needs to hire someone quickly for a specific period of time. Think twice before accepting a job under these circumstances. If you do take the job, be sure to negotiate your airfare home or at least back to the port of embarkation, and make tentative accommodation arrangements in case you have to return.
- Smaller yachts offer greater learning opportunities. This is because each crewmember is generally expected to do a lot of different jobs whereas on larger yachts with larger crews, the individual's responsibilities may be quite limited (and often boring).
- Longevity pays in this business just as it does in the 'real world'. You will be taken more seriously if you prove that you can stay put on the same boat for more than a few months. So, take care in choosing your jobs.

One of my former captains was fond of saying, *'You may get a job on a great boat, or with a great owner, or you may get great pay. If you get two of the three you've done well.'*

The following salary guide comes to us from Fred Dovaston Crew (www.yachtjob.com) based on their placement experience since January 2004. It gives approximate monthly salaries, in pounds sterling and in US dollars. Please note that these salaries are guidelines only, and that the above listed considerations should be taken into account as well. The US dollar is the most commonly used currency when negotiating salaries, even with yachts based in Europe, but since the dollar is currently very weak (I've used an exchange rate of £1.00:$1.81), European-based crew might prefer to negotiate their compensation in euros or pounds sterling.

AVERAGE MONTHLY SALARIES IN US DOLLARS (Jan 2004)

Yacht Size:	20-25m	25-35m	35-45m	45-55m	55-75m	75+m
Captain	3,500-6,000	4,000-8,000	6,000-10,000	8,000-12,000	10,000-15,000	13,000+
First mate	2,500-5,000		3,000-7,000	4,000-8,000	6,000-10,000	
Second mate/bosun				3,500-6,000	4,000-7,000	
Engineer (licensed)		3,500-6,000	4,000-7,000	5,000-9,000	7,000-10,000	
2nd engineer			3,500-6,000	4,000-8,000	6,000-9,000	
Deckhand	no exp 1,800-2,500 | exp & qualified 2,200-3,000 | excellent references 2,500-3,500					
Chef (trained)	experience with catering 3,000-5,000 | experience on yachts 3,500-5,000 |					
	proven record on yachts 5,000-7,000					
Cook	no formal training but proven capability 2,500-3,500					
Cook/steward	2,500-3,500					
Chief steward(ess)	exp as steward or 2nd steward 3,000-4,000 | proven record as chief steward 4,000-6,000					
Steward(ess)	no experience 2,000-2,500 | experienced 2,500-3,000 | excellent references 3,000-3,500					

AVERAGE MONTHLY SALARIES IN POUNDS STERLING (using $1.81:£1)

Yacht Size:	20-25m	25-35m	35-45m	45-55m	55-75m	75+m
Captain	1,935-3,315	2,210-4,420	3,315-5,525	4,420-6,630	5,525-8,287	7,182+
First mate	1,381-2,762		1,657-3,867	2,210-4,420	3,315-5,525	
Second mate/bosun				1,933-3,315	2,210-3,867	
Engineer (licensed)		1,934-3,315	2,210-3,867	2,762-4,972	3,867-5,525	
2nd engineer			1,934-3,315	2,210-4,420	3,315-4,972	
Deckhand	no exp 1,800-2,500 | exp & qualified 2,200-3,000 | excellent references 2,500-3,500					
Chef (trained)	experience with catering 1,657-2,762 | experience on yachts 1,934-2,762 |					
	proven record on yachts 2,762-3,867					
Cook	no formal training but proven capability 1,381-1,933					
Cook/steward	1,381-1,933					
Chief steward(ess)	exp as steward or 2nd steward 1,657-2,210 | proven record as chief steward 2,210-3,315					
Steward(ess)	no experience 1,105-1,381 | experienced 1,381-1,657 |excellent references 1,657-1,934					

JOB HUNTING

Preparing a CV

As with any job, you need to have a CV when applying for jobs aboard yachts. Putting together a CV or résumé may seem a daunting task, but even without prior yachting experience, most people have *some* experience or knowledge that can help land a job on a yacht.

* Have you worked in a restaurant? Experience in the kitchen, bar, or as a hostess or waiter is valuable aboard yachts.
* Do you speak more than one language? This is a *big* plus.
* Are you good with your hands? Do you have any wood-working experience?
* Are you mechanically inclined? Can you repair motors or electronics if necessary?

- Have you ever worked as a painter?
- Housekeeping experience is quite useful.
- Include *any* previous boating experience. Maybe you sailed dinghies or water-skied as a kid.
- If you learned to tie knots as a scout, include that too.
- An ability to entertain is highly prized. Can you play an instrument or sing? Can you juggle?
- Are you a qualified scuba diver?
- Flower arranging, much as skippers hate to admit it, is also an asset.
- Have you worked in an office? Bookkeeping experience or knowledge of computers can be an asset, though don't place the emphasis on this.

The ability to entertain the guests is a plus aboard a yacht where adverse weather can force everyone to stay in when they would rather be out.

Captains look for crew who will be pleasant to have on board. Crew accommodations are crowded, and crewmembers must work close to one another day in and day out. Therefore captains

Even childhood water sports training is worth a mention on your CV.

want 'team players'. Introverted or chronically depressed people don't last long in the yachting business.

Skippers also look for strong stomachs. You will be useless on a yacht if you cannot control the natural tendency towards seasickness. Everybody gets seasick occasionally, but a chronically seasick person is useless as a watchkeeper, useless as a cook, and makes everyone else's job harder. Put yourself to the test before you begin to apply for jobs. Go out on different types of boats. If you get sick the first time out, that's normal. Try again, and try the remedies listed later in the book. Even seasoned sailors get queasy sometimes. The question is whether you can override that queasy feeling and get on with your duties. If you really want to become a crewmember, you will find the strength to defeat seasickness.

All yachting CV's should include a head and shoulders photograph. You may include a digital photo directly in the heading. Or you may have passport photos taken and include one or two with each CV you send out. On my website, www.yachtie.net, I post CVs for prospective crew and one common mistake I see is that the photo submitted with the CV is often very poor. Have a good, professional looking photo of yourself taken. It's great if you can do it yourself, but if not, then find a shop that does passport photos. This is your first opportunity to impress your prospective employer.

When you apply for a job, you will need 2–3 letters of reference. These letters should describe some positive aspect of your character in addition to detailing your competence for the job that you held. If you have no letters of reference, call previous employers and get some. Even a character reference from a teacher is better than nothing. You may want to mention to the person writing the reference that some mention of your easygoing nature would be nice.

Crew placement agencies want paper copies of your CV along with an electronic copy on disk, CD or sent as an email attachment. If you are not able to do this yourself, hire a professional to format and type it. There are numerous résumé and CV preparation agencies listed on the Internet and in the telephone directories of most cities. First impressions are vitally important, and captains and owners of yachts, as businessmen, will appreciate the fact that you took the time to draft a professional looking document.

Chefs must include a 5 to 7 day sample menu and photos of their prepared foods.

There are examples for you to follow on the following pages. Be brief. CVs should be no longer than two pages. List past jobs chronologically, most recent first. Don't go back more than 10 years. It should not look like you omitted anything on purpose. If you have attended vocational college or university, you need not include information about your basic schooling.

(Sample) Curriculum Vitae

Donald Deckhand

Mailing address line #1
Mailing address line #2
Tel: (123) 456-7890 Mobile: (123) 456-7891
E-mail: donald@abc.com

Objective

Briefly describe your career goals. This should be relevant to the job for which you are applying. 3 – 4 sentences maximum. Include whether you prefer power or sailing yacht, what size vessel you prefer and waters you wish to cruise.

Licenses & Qualifications

List any licenses and qualifications that you hold which are relevant to the job for which you are applying. Include first aid certifications, and SCUBA licenses. If you have worked through many smaller certifications to attain larger ones, only include the larger ones.

Experience

Month, Year – Month Year position held
Name of yacht size of yacht / number of crew

- Served with Captain Whatever Hisname
- List duties performed.
- List special accomplishments
- Reason for leaving. (This is not always necessary.)
  Repeat this for as many jobs as necessary up to 10 years previous. May include non-marine jobs.

Education

Date Name of School or University City, State, Country
List degrees and honours earned.

Other Marine Experience

List any other maritime or pleasure boating experience, including military service, racing, sail training, scuba, wind surfing, etc.

Other Skills

List any skills that have not been mentioned already, like computer skills, other languages spoken, etc.

Interests

List special Interests and Hobbies.

References

List three recent references. Include their names, their positions, the company they work for and their contact info.

Sample Menu
Created by Kim Davis

❋
BREAKFAST

- Fresh fruit platter w/ selection of yoghurts
- Assorted fresh breads, muffins & pastries
- Walnut filled Belgian waffles
- Eggs florentine
- Huevos rancheros, salsa, chorizo & tortillas
- Broiled grapefruit w/ grand marnier flavoured French toast

❋
LUNCH

- West Indian pumpkin soup, frilled garlic prawns
- Crab tortellini w/ pesto, arugula salad w/cherry tomatoes
- Mozzarella pomadoro, prosciutto w/ melon, risotto milanese
- Green peppers stuffed w/ shrimp, herb-marinated tomatoes
- Chevre tarts w/ rosemary, spinach salad w/ bacon
- Broccoli soufflé in tomato shells, caesar salad

❋
APPETIZERS

- Salmon-nori hand rolls
- Sardines in puff pastry
- Manchego cheese straws
- Crostini w/ Tuscan pesto
- Mussels marinara
- Hot and sour lemon grass soup w/ straw mushrooms
- Lobster bisque

❋
ENTRÉES

- Hoisin glazed steak w/ scallion ginger slaw, Thai coconut rice, stir-fried asparagus
- Potato patties, almond crusted pork loin, sweet and sour small glazed onions, steamed carrots
- Pan grilled fish fillets, oven baked polenta, sautéed cherry tomatoes
- Roast rack of lamb, potatoes à la dauphinoise, steamed green beans and matchstick carrots w/ sesame oil
- Orange glazed game hens, rice stuffing w/ raisins & walnuts, broccoli florets
- Grilled lobster tails w/ garlic butter, spinach fettuccini alfredo, marinated tomato & cucumber

❋
DESSERTS

- Crepes Suzette w/ vanilla ice cream
- Pecan pie
- Rich chocolate cake w/ chocolate glaze
- Tiramisu
- Raspberry glace
- Lemon soufflé
- Mandel tart w/ lemon custard
- Mango crème brulée

Chef's food photo samples

Ideally these photos would be in colour and would be accompanied by a detailed menu.

Lunch for 8 aboard S/Y Amalthea of Sark June (date), Ibiza

Menu: Prosciutto with melon and walnuts, tea-stained quail eggs with smoked salmon and aioli; steamed asparagus; fresh tortellini with ricotta and parmesan, vine-ripened tomatoes and pesto.
Wine: Côte du Provence rosé.

Be sure to include one or two close-up photos.

Sample Letter of Reference

Redwood Investment Group Ltd.

Eastington Hall · Upton-upon-Severn · Worcestershire WR8 ORJ
Telephone 06846 4545 · Facsimile 06846 3686

DIRECTORS: *BARON HAMER OF ALFORD*
MICHAEL J. WAUGH F.C.A.

Redwood Investments Ltd.
Hampshire Securities Ltd.
Europa Properties Ltd.
Europa Investments Ltd.
Redwood Citrus Inc. (USA)
Europa Investments
  (Management) Ltd.
Hampshire Real Estate Ltd.
Barracuda Sailing Ltd. (CI)

TO WHOM IT MAY CONCERN

Kimberly PARISH DAVIS has been a crew member on board the Sailing Yacht AMALTHEA OF SARK for the past 20 months.

Kim has proved excellent in all aspects of her work, expecially fine cuisine. She is also an accomplished varnisher and as a professional seamstress makes all the curtains & covers for the boat.

On ocean passages, she is completely reliable on watch and always ready and willing to work on deck.

She is very honest, professional and personable and being also a musician of excellent voice, is very popular with the owners and guests.

Kim is highly recommended and I hope she will stay with the AMALTHEA OF SARK for many seasons to come.

R. McGowan —   YACHT AMALTHEA

_____
Richard McGOWAN-SCANLON
Captain AMALTHEA OF SARK

Redwood Investment Group Limited. Registered in England No. 1647692
Registered Office: Lincoln House · Basil Street · Knightsbridge · London SW3

Interview protocol

Once you have your CV, written references, copies of licenses and certifications, sample menu (if applicable) and pictures all done, take them to the copy shop and have at least 12 copies made of everything, and make at least that many digital copies on disc. Make up neat packets and have them stapled and ready to go, so you don't have to fumble around assembling all your bits and pieces when you get to the agent's office or meet a captain. You would be wise to get a waterproof folder to keep it all in. Not only does this ensure that your papers stay nice and clean, it will make you look a little more professional than if you appear with loose papers in hand.

Next, start calling on agencies and walking the docks. You can register with many agencies in advance online, which is convenient and shows that you are professional. You should still visit the agencies in person whenever you can. Make an appointment in advance.

Your appearance is very important as you begin interviewing. Make sure your hair and fingernails are clean and neatly trimmed. Girls, use a light hand with the makeup and tie your hair back if it is long. If you wear jewellery, keep it simple. A watch, a pair of small earrings and a necklace would be OK. It is best to downplay body piercing and tattoos. Wear clothes appropriate to the job. For example, navy blue, white or khaki trousers or shorts, white shirt and boat shoes would be ideal. Avoid T-shirts unless they are the pique golf shirt type with a collar.

Captains look for fresh, lively, energetic people with a positive attitude. Be tactful, and don't speak ill of a previous employer. The importance of a bright positive nature cannot be overstated, since attitudes are infectious. The last thing the captain wants is someone who is pessimistic or gossipy infecting the rest of his crew. Be confident, and prepare yourself to talk about where you've been and what you've been doing, and don't be afraid to ask questions including details about the pay and benefits package.

After you have visited the crew agencies, check in with them regularly. Pick one or two agents you feel comfortable with, and keep them posted about your movements. If you find a job on your own, let your agents know so they can take you out of their active files. Be courteous to these people, they can be your best friends, and they will remember you.

Day work

Day work – *work aboard any boat on which you are not a regular member of the crew. Day workers are generally paid in cash at the end of each day. The work could be just about anything, but usually involves cleaning, sanding, painting or varnishing.*

Even the highest and mightiest yacht skipper has at one time or another been reduced to the rank of 'day worker'. Let's take a look at what day working consists of, and how it can help you get going and keep going in the yachting industry.

Why you might get into day working
- Good day workers acquire reputations for doing good work, and get paid more as a result. Some people even prefer to stay in one place and day work. If you find a port where you want to settle down, day working can and will pay the rent.
- Day working can pay your expenses between jobs. This is important, since job security is a new concept in the yachting industry.
- Working on the boats as a day worker puts you in a position to hear of permanent jobs as they become available.
- Day working is an excellent way to break into the business. You make important contacts. People get to know your face, and your work. It's OK to ask for instructions as long as you follow them.
- Some day working jobs carry on long enough that you can ask for a letter of recommendation.

- Day work can lead to a permanent crew position, since it is a risk free trial period for a skipper to see if you suit his requirements.

A few reasons why a captain might hire a day worker

- On the smaller yachts, if there is a nasty job the captain doesn't want to do himself, he'll hire a day worker. Some examples are: bilge cleaning, stripping and sanding varnish, polishing stainless steel or brass, cleaning masts and rigging, cleaning waterlines, diving to clean the bottom of the boat and the propeller, or if the boat is out of the water, painting the bottom. Insist on a proper safety mask and skin protection. Read the label on whatever paint or chemical you've been asked to apply if you are uncertain about the precautions you need to take. Marine paints are full of dangerous chemicals.
- If there is a big job to do. For example, if there is a lot of varnishing to be done day workers may be needed.
- If there is a lot of cleaning to do and not a lot of time. For example the yacht owner has announced that he is arriving in three days, and the boat has just completed a long charter or ocean crossing. The captain will likely hire day workers to help. Anything and everything on the boat will be cleaned, and hours will be long. If at all possible, a coat of varnish will be splashed around as well. (Owners are not generally aware of the chaos their impromptu visits cause!)

How to find day work

- Walk the docks and visit boatyards and dry-docks early in the morning, before 8:00 am, since captains like to get their crews going by 8:00.
- Hang out where the professional crew eat and drink, and make it known that you're looking for work. There is generally a marina cantina and 'happy hour', when everyone is finishing for the day, is the ideal time to meet new people. Be brave. If you must tell people you've never done this before, let them know that you are a quick learner and a hard

Don't discount the small 'do-it-yourself' yards when looking for day work.

worker. If you think you can fake it, go for it, but major blunders will be big news within minutes so it is sometimes wise to admit that you need instructions. (I am reminded of the Italian chap who told us he knew all about a two-part varnish we wanted him to use on our bowsprit. He didn't, and it took us two days to correct his mistake. We told everyone we knew not to hire him.)

♦ Check with the local yacht brokers and crew placement agencies. Let them know that you will take day work until a permanent position comes up. You could land a boat-cleaning job that will run indefinitely. Many of the agencies have quite a few boats to maintain for prospective buyers.

♦ Print up some business cards. You can get 250 for only the cost of shipping from www.vistaprint.com. I started out with 100 cards that said *'Kim Cleans Boats'* and listed my phone number. People all over Ft Lauderdale knew me as 'Kim Cleansboats'. I had four places that I visited daily looking for work. I rarely went a day without work. I carried on that way for a couple of months riding my bicycle between the docks and the boatyards, and eventually my day working lead to my first permanent crew position.

◆ Don't discount the smaller 'do-it-yourself' yards. They are easier to get into, and quite often you'll find a stressed out yacht owner very happy to hire you to assist with his boat's repairs.

Deliveries

Deliveries are contract positions that require you to help move a boat from one place to another. Once you arrive at the destination, the job is over. Paid delivery crew should get return tickets to their port of embarkation. (Always check before you set out to make sure that your air fare home will be provided in addition to your pay.)

There are also unpaid deliveries, where you simply gain experience and a free ride. However, when you are new, the thing you need most of all is experience. There is a lot of delivery work to be done, and it is worth keeping in mind as you start out. Many yacht brokers employ delivery skippers regularly to move boats from one boat show to another, and to deliver the boats they've sold to their new owners. If you make friends with a busy delivery skipper, you can learn a lot about yachting in a hurry without having to be on your best behaviour for guests. Don't forget to visit yacht sales offices when you start your job-hunt, since they generally know the delivery skippers in the area.

Crew accommodation

This excerpt comes from a recent e-mail I had from one of my 'informants' in Ft Lauderdale, Florida:

I've been busy day working, mainly cleaning – both interior and exterior. The going rate for day workers is between $12 and $15 US per hour. Lunch and transportation should be included.

I've found most of my jobs via the crew house – we get calls all the time and sometimes captains stop in. The Neptune Group has a good reputation for getting calls. I've also met people at Waxy's – Friday nights are big for captains and crew hanging out. I haven't done a lot of walking the docks.

As far as crew house etiquette goes, it is important for people to tidy up after themselves. We've had a couple of slobs living in our house and they were very unpopular. One roomate of mine brought two huge suitcases stuffed with tons of clothes and had her 'kit' everywhere. I can't imagine how she would get along sharing crew quarters on a yacht – and she is interested in a stew job! Even the majority of the guys get annoyed when people leave their dirty dishes in the sink or worse don't even bother to put their dirty dishes in the sink. I know it sounds obvious but just being tidy and respectful goes a long way.

I receive many requests for information about crew housing, so with that in mind, here is a listing of the crew houses and hostels I've found to date.

Ft Lauderdale, Florida

There are several good online lists of crew houses:
* www.crewfinders.com/house.html
* www.crewbydrwoods.com/linksresources.housing.cfm
* www.americaninstitute.com/crewhousing/

New Port, Rhode Island

* The Poplar House: Walter – +1 (401) 846 0976
* Crewfinders' summer office: see Toni Brooks for a referral – +1 (401) 849 5227
* Jackie's Crew Housing: +1 (401) 662 0848

South of France

- The Crew House, 1 Ave St Roch, 06600 Antibes, Tel: +33 (0) 4 9290 4939 Fax: +33 (0)4 9290 4938 Email: workstationfr@yahoo.com
- You'll find numerous locations in Nice at www.hostels europe.com
- Antibes Youth Hostel, Caravelle 60, Boulevard de la Garoupe, 06600 Antibes, Tel: +33 (0) 4 93 61 34 40 Fax: +33 (0) 4 93 42 72 57
- Hotel Teranga, 5, Rue Marcel Paul, Antibes, Juan les Pins – see listing at www.europeanexplorer.com
- Relais International de la Jeunesse, Blvd de la Mer, Cap D'Ail, Tel: +33 (0) 4 93 78 18 58

Palma de Mallorca, Spain

All these hostels were found at www.hostelseurope.com and you can book your stay online there.
- Can Pastilla Hostel, Ortage 4, Can Pastilla, Palma de Mallorca
- Hostel Colon, 31 Desembre, Palma de Mallorca
- Terramar, Plaza Mediterraneo 8, Palma de Mallorca

Around the world

- www.studentabroad.com
- www.Hostelworld.com
- www.Backpacker-UK.com
- www.EuropeanExplorer.com
- www.bugeurope.com

HEALTH ISSUES

No job, however fun or glamorous is worth risking your health. That is why you need to take some precautions before you set out on your new career afloat.

Health Insurance

When you get a job on a boat, your employer must provide health insurance but you might need to top it up!. Many of the beautiful and exotic places yachts frequent have substandard hospitals and inept doctors. If you need medical attention, don't let lack of funds cost you your life. You can't afford to save money on this.

A good mariner's health insurance policy will pay for world-wide coverage including medical evacuation if it should ever be required. Up to the age of 40, most people can get good health coverage for less than $100 US per month. Once you get a job, make sure the captain has a copy of your insurance policy in case of emergency. Your crew placement agent will probably direct you to a good insurance company, but if not here are some companies where you can enquire:

Insure and Go
Offers backpackers travel insurance
Web: www.insureandgo.com

Quote Travel Insurance
Web:http:// quotetravelinsurance.com

MHG Marine Benefits – MHG Associates
1041 SE 17th Street
Suite 207
Ft. Lauderdale
FL 33316
USA
Tel: +1 (954) 828 1819
Fax: +1 (954) 760 9033
Email:
yachts@mhgmarine.com
Web: www.mhgmarine.com

International Medical Group Inc
Marine Crew Benefits
Department
407 Fulton Street
Indianapolis
Indiana 46202-3684
USA
Tel: +1 (317) 655 4500
or (800) 628 4664
Fax: +1 (317) 655 4505

Email:
insurance@imglobal.com
Web: www.imglobal.com

In the UK:

IMG Europe Ltd
36-38 Church Road
Burgess Hill
West Sussex RH15 9AE
Tel: +44 (0) 1444 465577
Fax: +44 (0) 1444 465550

Crew Insurance Associates Inc
Chuck Bortell –
General Agent
5200 N Federal HWY
Suite 2
Ft Lauderdale
FL 33308
USA
Tel: +1 (954) 491 3422
Fax: +1 (954) 772 8740
Email:
info@yachtcrewinsurance.com
Web:
www.yachtcrewinsurance.com

RYC & JH Palm Beach
(Group and individual crew
insurance worldwide)
2716 South Dixie Highway
West Palm Beach
FI 33405
USA
Tel: +1 (561) 366 8666
Fax: +1 (561) 366 8606
Email: palmbeach@
    rivierayacht.com
Web: http://rivierayacht.com

Nutrition and Preventive Maintenance

One of the perks of working on a yacht is that a chef prepares the meals. If you eat the food that is provided, you can be sure of getting a balanced diet. Consider taking vitamin and mineral supplements anyway. The schedule can be quite hectic for yacht crews, and it is rarely convenient for anyone to take a sick day. Many scientists today claim that even with an optimal diet, we don't get all the vitamins and minerals we need due to soil depletion, genetic engineering and chemical additives.

In particular, minerals may be lacking in the water aboard yachts. Reverse osmosis often supplies the ship's drinking water. This leaves the water tasteless and devoid of minerals. Deck and engineering crew in particular, need to take care that they get enough minerals to replenish what they perspire away since they have to work in extremely hot conditions and sweat profusely.

Getting enough fibre in your diet is also vital. With the hectic schedule of the typical crewmember, irregularity and constipation are common. Nobody likes to talk about this, but it can be a serious problem, allowing dangerous toxins to build up in

You can't afford to get sick – so think ahead.

your body. If you already have chronic constipation, or if it develops once you start working on yachts, consider taking a mild natural laxative to keep everything moving. A healthy adult should have at least one bowel movement per day. Look for a product that will not cause cramping or discomfort.

Seasickness

Most professional sailors feel seasick from time to time, but we don't like to admit it. In fact we used to make great sport of the seasick tourists when I worked on the catamarans in St Maarten. We would gather around the dinner table after a hard day entertaining day-trippers and compare seasick stories. Usually one passenger would have started it off, and before you knew it you were handing plastic bags around to all 20-odd passengers. It paid to know the flight schedules from St Barth's back to St Maarten. Of course we never told the guests about the runway in St Barth's.

Motion sickness is the result of the eyes, the sensory nerves, and the inner ear sending conflicting signals to the brain. Age, heredity, stress, poor ventilation, and travelling on a full stomach may also contribute to an individual's susceptibility.

As long as you know what to look out for, most cases of *mal de mer* can be controlled, and it is easier to prevent than to treat after it has started. Sensible eating before and during cruising along with using medication correctly and following some simple behaviour guidelines will save most people from having to bend over that dreaded bucket.

People generally gain their sea legs within 48–72 hours, however the nausea can come back again if the motion of the boat changes. Sufferers feel fine again as soon as they get to calm water. If it is possible to go for a swim, this alleviates the nausea almost instantly.

The hull shape of certain boats can exaggerate seasickness, so just because you got sick on a deep sea fishing trip when you were 12 years old does not mean that you will feel ill on a luxury yacht with stabilisers. Here are some basics to help prevent seasickness:

- Don't eat a spicy or greasy meal before you set out. Even a very rich meal the day before can aggravate the tendency to feel sick.
- Don't drink alcohol.
- Try to stay on deck as near the middle of the boat as possible, this reduces the motion. Don't be coerced into doing a job below decks, especially not in the galley or engine room.
- Don't drink a lot of coffee or tea before you set out. Since these are diuretics, they will send you to the head, and you want to avoid that enclosed little space when you first set out.
- Don't move around too much, and if you are below decks, lie down.
- Try focusing on a distant object on the horizon when you're on deck.
- Avoid watching a moving object like the compass.
- It will help to take your mind off your nausea if you can find

something to do like steering the boat. (For this you can look at the compass occasionally!)

♦ Sit to windward if you're on deck, or near an electric fan if you're below deck.

♦ Don't read.

♦ Breathe deeply and close your eyes. (This helps by limiting the conflicting stimuli.)

♦ Avoid strong odours, especially diesel fumes!

♦ Whatever you do, *don't dwell on the feeling of nausea!*

♦ Watch for lethargy, yawning, headache, flatulence, drowsiness, and pale clammy skin. These are some of the symptoms you may experience before actually feeling nausea or vomiting. A winning strategy at this point is to take a nap. If you actually begin to vomit, don't fight it. You'll feel better when it passes. Then take your nap. Also, if you are ill, use a bucket or bag. It is not safe to lean over the side.

Now suppose all that good advice has failed. There are a variety of drugs on the market. All the tablets have one obvious failing. Most people don't take a tablet until they feel ill, by which time it is too late. The tablet rarely has a chance to dissolve before it is brought back up. *Take your seasickness pills 6–8 hours before you set out.* Here is a sampling of the different motion sickness remedies on the market. The stronger preparations require a prescription, and as with all medications, you should check with your doctor anyway before taking them:

♦ **Cinnarizine (Stugeron®)** – This British drug is very popular among cruisers. It is effective in all conditions, and it is sold in many countries around the world, particularly those with ties to Britain. The brand name may be different. It is not available in the US or Canada.

♦ **Dextroamphetamine (Dexedrine®)** – An amphetamine laced preparation that works in extreme conditions. Available in long and short-term preparations.

- **Dimenhydrinate (Dramamine®, Gravol®)** – This common over-the-counter drug is available in plain tablets, chewable tablets, long-acting capsules, syrup, suppositories, and injectable preparations. It may cause drowsiness and feelings of vertigo, and is not very effective in heavy weather conditions.
- **Meclizine (Bonamine®, New Dramamine®)** – This works as long as it is not too rough, but it may cause drowsiness.
- **Promethazine (Phenergan®)** – Pills, liquid, and suppositories are available. Phenergan works in severe conditions, but causes extreme drowsiness, therefore it is taken in conjunction with **Ephedrine**. This 'Navy Cocktail' was developed for the space programme. Suppositories are useful if vomiting has already begun. Be sure to read the warnings on anything with Ephedrine in it, since there are potentially serious side effects for people with high blood pressure and heart conditions.
- **Scopolomine patch (Transderm V®)** Scopolamine patches are very popular because they work for 72 hours, and continue to work once the person is already sick. However, they are expensive and the patch must be applied 8 hours prior to setting out. Scopolamine patches require a prescription, and they should not be used by anyone with glaucoma.

If you prefer natural remedies: try fresh ginger. The traditional method is to chew the fresh root, but I prefer to make an infusion by boiling slices of the fresh root. The infusion is good to use before you set out, but it is also good for the green ones who are sick already. Add a little honey to sweeten it. Or you can buy ginger tablets. Take 1000 milligrams every three hours, starting one hour before setting out. Crystallized ginger sweets are quite civilized as well. Other natural remedies include:

- **Charcoal tablets** – take 5, one hour before travel. Do not take them with other medicines or supplements.
- **Magnesium** – 500 mg, one hour before the trip acts as a nerve tonic.

- **Vitamin B6** – 100 mg, one hour before the trip, then 100 mg two hours later will relieve nausea.
- **Peppermint** – the tea soothes the stomach. A drop of the oil on the tongue relieves nausea, and it may also be taken in lozenge form.
- **Papaya tablets** – the chewable ones are useful for all manner of gastric discomfort.
- **Homeopathic liver remedy** – may reduce nausea since nausea may be indicative of liver problems.
- **Pressure-point bands** – these are sold in drugstores under various names. They work on Chinese acupuncture principles. Many people have success with them.
- **TravelWell** – this is an audio program being advertised on the Internet. It claims to offer travel sickness relief. The manufacturers claim that it is safe and effective, even for pregnant women and children. They also claim that it is currently in use by 50% of the teams on the BT Global Challenge Yacht Race. Look it up at www.travelwell.co.uk.

Don't stop eating if you've been sick. Have an apple. It will get rid of the bad taste in your mouth and give you energy to go on fighting. Fruit moves through our systems very quickly, especially when unimpeded, and gives us lots of very good vitamins and nutrients with very little work on the part of our digestive systems. And apples don't taste sour on the way back up!

Do eat fruit and vegetables, and as any pregnant woman will tell you, dry crackers help once you feel green. Olives will also ward off nausea since they decrease salivation. Make sure to drink plenty of fresh water and fruit juice to combat dehydration, but avoid citrus juices as the acid will aggravate an upset stomach.

Skin Cancer

There is no denying the fact that if you work on a boat your risk of developing skin cancer will increase. This need not be a problem as long as you know what to watch for. There are two types of skin cancer:

- **Non-melanoma** (basal and squamous cell carcinoma) which has a 95% cure rate when found early and treated properly.
- **Melanoma** which can be quite deadly if it goes undetected.

Prevention is the best protection. Overexposure to the sun's rays is the main cause of skin cancer, especially when it results in blistering sunburn. People with fair skin are most susceptible, but anyone can develop skin cancer. Most skin cancers can be prevented with appropriate use of sun protection, which sounds simple enough, but in practice the following expert advice is pretty hard to follow when you are working in the hot tropical sun every day.

Experts say that a broad-spectrum (UVA and UVB) sun block with a sun protection factor (SPF) of 15 or more should be applied every two hours when you are outdoors. In addition to using sun block, wear tight weave dark clothing made of natural fabrics, hats, and broad-spectrum sunglasses. Try not to be out side in the mid-day sun.

Early detection is very important, especially in the marine industry, and periodic self-examination of skin spots is not only recommended, it is essential. My Spanish doctor made this helpful suggestion:

- Have your spouse or a very close friend make a list of *all* the moles and suspicious spots on your body.
- *Then* see the doctor and have him check the ugliest ones.
- Save the list, because you'll want to use it for comparison the next year when you repeat the procedure, making special note of the moles that have changed or grown.

Most spots on your skin, like freckles, birthmarks, and moles are normal. Melanomas can be recognized by following the ABCD's:

♦ **A**symmetry (no matching halves when split in the middle)
♦ **B**orders that are irregular, notched, or scalloped
♦ **C**olours that vary with different tones of brown, tan, black, and/or white
♦ **D**iameter larger than the size of a pencil eraser (6mm or 1/4 inch)

If you think you may have a melanoma, see a dermatologist as soon as possible.

Exercise

Getting enough exercise is a challenge for anyone working on a yacht. On sailing vessels, the deck crews have a tendency to have over-developed upper bodies, and wimpy under-developed legs. On all yachts, the on-duty hours are long, and when you are on charter you have to fight for time to yourself. When you do get a few hours off, the last thing you think of doing is exercising. Top that off with the fact that you generally eat rich foods accompanied by too much wine.

However, with a little effort it is possible to make time for exercise. Here are some suggestions:

♦ When the boat is at anchor, swim laps around it.
♦ When the boat is at the dock, take a walk or run in the after-noon or evening. (Don't stop for ice cream or beer!)
♦ When there are no guests on board, go hiking, or look for a stable that rents horses.
♦ Buy a set of strap-on weights and do basic strength training exercises on deck. Include leg lifts, squats, push-ups and sit-ups. Start with just a few repeats and build up gradually.

Swimming around the boat at anchor is a great way to exercise,
and you get to experience the local marine life.

- There is usually room somewhere on deck for some simple yoga routines, like the 'sun salutation'.
- Or find a secluded beach for sunbathing, swimming and yoga.

SHARING SMALL SPACES

What to take

Your storage space on the boat will be limited to one small cupboard (or locker). All of your belongings will have to fit there, including your luggage. So pack light using a cloth duffel bag. You should also be able to carry everything in one trip if you are travelling through airports between jobs. A large duffel bag and a small backpack should suffice. Most of the time you will be in uniform or in a bathing suit, so you don't need much. If you are a musician, think hard about whether or not to subject your favourite guitar to life at sea. It may be better to wait until you have a job that looks like it will last for a few years (preferably with a big cabin to yourself!).

Here are the basics:

- Underwear, enough for a week (a lot of deckhands seem to think they don't need underwear – wrong! There are many places on a boat where you can accidentally get a look up someone's shorts…)
- Two pairs of pyjamas or nightgowns
- Three or four swimsuits
- Three T-shirts
- One short sleeve dress shirt or blouse
- One long sleeve shirt or blouse
- 1–2 sweaters, or sweatshirts *300*
- 3–4 pairs of shorts
- 1–2 pairs of jeans
- One pair of trousers, (or ladies) one skirt
- One pair of sandals or flip-flops
- One pair of deck shoes
- Three pairs of socks
- Two pairs of sunglasses (in case you lose one)
- One folding hat or cap
- *Optional: 1 pair dress shoes, 1 pair hiking boots, one sport coat or blazer*
- Take your own toothpaste, shampoo, shaving cream and razors. The boat may supply these, but don't expect it when you first start.
- Girls don't forget ample feminine supplies

Avoiding embarrassing situations

This section covers a number of simple things that experienced *400* crewmembers take for granted. Every one of the things listed here has come up either with me or with someone I know. Some of this stuff is really personal, and that is why I am including it. Other people may find it hard to say directly to you.

I am assuming we all wash daily and brush our teeth at least twice a day!

- Always ask the captain's permission before bringing guests on board.
- Always coil sheets, lines, and water hoses in a clockwise direction.
- The sheets go around the drum on the winch in a clockwise direction. Winch handling is serious business. If you are fond of all your fingers, take the time to learn how to do this properly. See Appendix 3 for useful photos.
- Fingernails and toenails should be trimmed or filed in private. Hands and nails need to be immaculate, but don't let the guests see you grooming them (this is especially true for the chef).
- There may not be a lot of privacy in the crew quarters. Wear discreet sleepwear. Even if you are not bashful about nudity, your crewmates may not want to know all your secrets!
- When showering, keep in mind that water supplies are limited. You must not run the water non-stop for the entire shower. The same is true for tooth brushing. Here is the way a shower should be done on a yacht: *get wet, turn the water off, shampoo hair and lather skin, turn water on long enough to rinse off all soap.*
- Wipe down the entire head following your shower, and try not to leave any hair in the soap! You'll be sharing that small shower with the rest of the crew, and it is no fun to shower after a woolly mammoth or a slob.
- In a pinch, baby wipes work wonders for a quick touch up. They even clean grease off dirty hands. Keep a box on hand for your own personal use.
- Salt water does not react well with perm-treated or coloured hair. If green is not your intended colour, rinse with fresh water as soon as possible.
- Hairstyles on board should not require much attention. If your style requires a hairdryer and lots of touch-ups, consult your hairdresser about a new 'do'. Wind and sea spray are a fact of life, even on a luxury yacht, and you will not have time to worry about what your hair is doing.

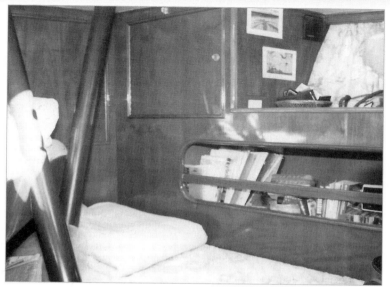

Home sweet home – if you're lucky, you might get an entire locker to yourself.

- Don't leave dirty clothes lying around the crew quarters. There is nothing more disgusting than someone else's smelly underwear or swimming trunks abandoned in a heap in the middle of the floor.

- Use the toilet brush when you flush. Skid marks in the bowl are almost as bad as an incomplete flush. These are the sort of 'presents' we'd rather our crew mates did not leave for us.

- Speaking of flushing, *nothing* should ever be flushed down the marine toilet (head) that you did not eat or drink first. Toilet paper is usually allowed, but don't use more than absolutely necessary. Please read the section on 'heads' later in this chapter.

Housekeeping tips for chef and steward

- All galley surfaces and crevices must be cleaned after every meal.
- Before discarding food packaging, especially from meats, wash it to avoid creating smelly garbage. This goes for tins as well.
- Make sure the milk is in a tightly-sealed carton. Emptying and cleaning the bottom of the refrigerator is a pain.
- Keep lots of extra small plastic garbage bags – unscented. They come in handy if a guest is seasick. Tie a knot in the top and throw the bag away. (Crew can use the 'bucket and chuck it' method – they can generally be trusted not to fall overboard when they empty the bucket. The same cannot be said for guests.)
- Buy soap that does not foam excessively. The object here is to minimize soap scum build-up in the pipes and holding tanks. You only need one whiff of an open holding tank to understand why I stress this point.
- Every few days scrub the shower grates with a brush to remove soap scum and hair. To do this quickly, just turn them over and scrub them in situ, rinsing with the showerhead. Between charters, take them out on the dock and do a more thorough job.
- Remove hair from drains daily.
- Empty all garbage bins daily, and take all rubbish ashore if at all possible.
- It may take some practice if the bunks are odd shapes, but try to keep the bed linens tucked in so tightly that there are no wrinkles. In a pinch, you can actually iron the sheets right on the beds.
- Always tie your hair back when cooking. Even if you know it is clean, your guests will not be impressed if they find hair in the soufflé.
- Never stick your fingers in the food.

66

- Never taste from the spoon you're cooking with. Use a clean one every time. You simply cannot chance spreading any germs.
- All cuts and sores must be covered, especially in the galley. Blue adhesive bandages are recommended for cooks. If one should come off in the food, it's easy to find. (Ugh!)
- If you have a cold, wear a mask when cooking. Unfortunately, it is not easy to get a day off when the boat is chartering or when the owner is on board. If you really are too sick to cook, make sure you've trained someone else to prepare at least one passable meal.
- Always give the guests bottled water to keep beside their bunks and to brush teeth with. The last thing you want is for your guests to get diarrhoea from drinking tainted water.
- Make your ice, coffee, and tea using bottled water, or water produced using a watermaker. Make sure it tastes OK. Never trust water from the dock. Just be sure to take a mineral supplement if you are using water produced with a reverse osmosis watermaker.
- Everyone, lord and labourer alike, must remove their street shoes as they come on board. There should be a shoe basket waiting at one end of the gangway. If guests want to wear shoes while they are on deck, they'll have to have a pair especially for use on board.
- Have a deck shower set up whenever anyone goes to the beach. You'll be sorry if you let them bring *any* sand on the boat, because you'll chase it forever, and never get rid of it.
- It will pay you to develop an introductory speech about how the head works. You cannot impress upon the guests enough the importance of not putting *anything* down the head that hasn't been down their gullets first!
- If you have the space for it, get a wet/dry shop vacuum for when the head does block. It's still a nightmare to clean up, but being able to remove the left-overs from the bowl quickly while holding your nose with one hand helps a lot.
- Buy *lots* of tea towels. The towel in use should always look and smell fresh, even if you have to change it 10 times a day.

It's a terrible shame to spoil the nose on a good wine because the glass was dried with a smelly rag.

- When making beds, remove your rings to avoid scratching the varnish.

- When working in the galley, wear an apron and keep a spare. You'll often have to pop up to see the guests while still cooking. This way your clothes stay presentable.

- Clean the floor on hands and knees unless you're on a very large yacht. It's quicker, since you can combine the sweeping and mopping and just wipe down once. Vinegar water in a spray bottle works well for varnished floors and bulkheads, but be prepared for the smell.

- Never leave or enter a port with laundry drying on the life lines!

- Bleach and white vinegar are essential cleaners that are available wherever you go. Just avoid using them until your guests go ashore, since they have overpowering odours.

- Start the toilet roll whenever you put a new one out. (No one likes fighting that glue at the beginning – and a neat little point folded into the end looks very posh. It also makes it clear that you have been there and cleaned the head.)

- Wipe down all the surfaces in the guest heads every day several times. It's a good idea to keep a chamois and a squeegee in each head. Depending on how formal your boat is, you can sometimes instruct your guests to wipe everything down following their showers.

- Ordinary window cleaner works well on all bathroom surfaces for a quick clean and polish, and it does not leave any residue.

Heads

Today's yachts have one thing in common with the space shuttle. Millions of dollars have been spent on research and development, and years have been devoted to testing and feedback, still neither has a reliable toilet system.

There are many types of yacht heads (marine toilets). They range from the classic hand pump type (great for the upper body), to electric vacuum and pump types. But whether it is manually operated or electric, the head must get waste from the bowl to the holding tank. The problem is that in most cases the toilet and the plumbing are situated below the waterline. So in order to keep the waste flowing in the desired direction, the plumbing gets very complicated. The typical system involves one-way valves, pumps, sea cocks, pipes, switches, wiring, gaskets etc. In other words, an awful lot of things can go wrong, and they do.

You will see this slogan posted on most boats, 'If you didn't eat it or drink it, it doesn't go in this toilet!' There is a good reason for this. You will be amazed at how easily the marine toilet can block. A lock of hair or even multi-ply toilet paper will block some heads.

There is no getting around the fact that one day you will be present when a head blocks. Go directly to the captain, first mate or engineer and let them know that a head is blocked. It will have to be dealt with, and all the officers will be familiar with how this is done. Clearing blocked heads is the most despised job at sea, and they always seem to block at the most inopportune moments. If you are very lucky, you will not be asked to help with the repairs! The main thing is to make sure you follow the rules about what can be put down the head, and keep in mind that these infernal machines all block periodically, so it is most likely not your fault.

Get over any embarrassment about this subject because like everyone else, you will be expected to educate guests about using the head. Anytime a guest comes onboard, escort them to the toilet the first time and give them a quick explanation. Every boat is a little different and it can sometimes be a real challenge to figure out how to work a strange head. Some older models of marine toilet require that you depress a pedal or button for several seconds in order to completely clear the bowl. I am convinced that yacht designers take perverse delight in hiding the magic button that flushes the blasted things. Be nice and spare your guests the agony of trying to figure it out themselves.

POTENTIAL PROBLEMS TO AVOID

Wear your safety gear

Most of the time, cruising yachts travel around in fair weather entertaining their guests in a civilized fashion with champagne and caviar. However, Mother Nature is fickle. Squalls come up suddenly at sea and in the space of a few minutes the weather can change dramatically. All the members of the crew sometimes have to work on deck in nasty weather. The yacht should provide safety harnesses and lifejackets for everyone. The ocean is not a place to worry about whether or not you look cool in your lifejacket. Wear it.

Though we all practice man overboard drills to the point where we think we could do them in our sleep, the truth is that in a real man overboard situation, it is very difficult to get the boat turned around fast enough to keep sight of the person in the water. Hence it is extremely difficult to affect a successful rescue. Even in tropical water, our fragile human bodies can succumb to hypothermia in just 20 minutes. So, going overboard is a very big deal.

Another fact that is not widely known by landlubbers is that many men go overboard while having a quick whiz over the side. Chaps, it sounds stupid, I know, but this is not a joke. Is that really the way you want to lose your life? Just use the head like the rest of us, OK?

And while we're talking about safety, always remember to coil sheets, lines, and water hoses in a clockwise direction. The water hose probably won't hurt you, but sheets and lines can save your life if they run freely as they should, or they can take your life or your limbs if you get tangled in them. This may sound like an exaggeration, but things have a way of happening very quickly on boats and you often have no time to deal with tangled lines.

The sheets go around the winch drum in a clockwise direction. Winch handling is a serious business. If you are fond of all your fingers, take the time to learn how to do this properly using a real sheet and a real winch. Get someone to show you how to take in slack quickly and safely and then have them show you how to let the tension off a sheet safely. If you simply let go of the off-side sheet when tacking, anyone on deck could be seriously injured by the flogging sheet that results. This is one of the most important things you need to know when you starting out on sailing yachts. Don't try to bluff your way through this, it is too important. (See the illustrations in Appendix 3.)

Couples on yachts

There is no denying that people sometimes meet and fall in love (or lust) within the yachting community. I met my husband while we were working on two different boats in a Miami boatyard. So, being a romantic at heart, I can't tell you to take

Working as a couple presents special challenges.

vows of chastity when you go to work on a yacht. I do, however, feel compelled to tell you that working as a couple in the yachting industry presents special challenges.

Many skippers will not hire couples. The reasons for this go way back, but let's suffice it to say that emotional situations make people behave irrationally, which leads to trouble among the crew. You are more likely to find yourself dating someone who works on a different boat. Then what do you do? Hope your schedules coincide? Look for a job where you can be together? The answers are not simple. Patience is the key. You need to prove to yourselves and everyone else that your relationship is stable, and that neither of you is going to act stupidly because of it. Don't expect your captain to get excited about hiring someone you met in a bar last week.

There are some jobs that are well suited for couples, but these generally require that one partner be a licensed captain, while the other is an experienced chef or stew. A couple who have been married for a while will have a much better chance of being hired together because they have proven that their relationship is not going to break up and disrupt the cruising season.

The problem for married couples is that owners don't want them to procreate. As a couple interviewing for a job with the owner of a yacht, be prepared to explain how you either don't want children, or plan to wait five or 10 years before you have any.

Sexual harassment

Aboard a yacht, the temptation to touch or speak to a guest or co-worker in a provocative manner can be overwhelming, but as a professional crewmember on a superyacht, discretion is one of the key attributes you must cultivate. Be careful using sexual innuendo, even at sea where gorgeous people wander around wearing almost nothing all the time. If you can't keep your comments to yourself, you may find yourself on the dock with no place to sleep.

Sadly, even in the 21st century, it is still necessary to remind young crewmembers to be careful who they sail with. Although

Keep your hands and comments to yourself at all times!

conditions are improving as everyone becomes more aware of sexual harassment as a problem, there is still the potential for serious trouble at sea. Take care especially on smaller boats and deliveries. An unscrupulous captain of our acquaintance was fond of taking young women on deliveries and demanding sexual favours once the boat was out of sight of land. He threatened to throw them overboard if they did not comply. Be smart. Crimes at sea are hard to prove…

Remember why you're there

Always keep in mind that your primary objective is to see that your guests have a good time. This is not always easy. Some people are a pleasure to serve, while others are not. If the guests have been on a yacht before, half the work is done for you. People new to yachting who arrive with a positive attitude are always welcome as well. But there will be many others who present special challenges.

Older people who arrive full of enthusiasm, but with limited mobility provide one example of unusually trying guests you may meet. You'll be involved in arranging special procedures to help them on and off the boat, and assist them getting from place to place while they are onboard. Ideally, the captain will have had some warning about any special needs of this sort, and arrangements will already be in place to accommodate them.

The most common miserable guests you will encounter are the wives of keen sailors who do not enjoy sailing themselves. Often they hate the sun, the sea, and anything that messes up their hair. You will need to understand that these women are not on the yacht because they want to be there. If they act grumpy, try not to take offence. Their bad mood is not usually directed at you. You just happen to be in the line of fire. Sometimes all you can do with these poor women is to smile and say 'no problem' when they make difficult requests.

*Children can be a joy to have on board
if they are allowed to play along the way.*

Once you understand your guests, you'll be able to decide what is needed to make their stay as enjoyable as possible. Take into account your guests' ages, physical condition, and personalities. What are their expectations? Do they want to fish, sail, go fast, get a suntan, go snorkelling or swimming, or do they just want to brag that they've been on a yacht? Watch to make sure that they are content. Sometimes people will suffer in silence, and if an observant crewmember can recognize that there is a problem brewing it can save the guest hours or even days of discomfort. It will help with tips as well.

In the case of charter guests, the charter broker should have provided a preference sheet filled out by the guests when they booked their trip. This questionnaire will give you some clues about what the guests expect, including food and drink preferences, but until you meet them, you won't know what they are really like. The captain will phone prospective guests a week or two before their scheduled arrival to clear up any last minute details or changes of plan. That will be the opportune time for him to remind them to take motion sickness pills before they arrive.

Not everyone knows what is appropriate on a yacht. For example, when they first arrive you'll have to explain to the guests that everyone must take their shoes off as they come on board. Be good-natured about this. An introductory memo for all guests that details the 'do's and don'ts' of the yacht is very helpful. Leave a copy of this memo in each cabin, and make sure that the guests read it.

Each guest should be shown how to work the head as soon as possible. Have them do a practice flush, and be precise about the amount of toilet paper to be used. With women, be explicit: absolutely no sanitary products are to be flushed.

Show them where the bathroom disposal bin is, and make sure that there is a bin liner in it at all times and that it is emptied regularly. Hopefully this will discourage sneak flushers.

You need to be able to show guests around the boat and explain all safety equipment and procedures without scaring them into thinking the boat is going to sink. Make sure each one has a 'personal flotation device' or lifejacket.

The easiest guests to entertain are the ones who want to participate. The captain and first mate can help by assigning simple tasks while the boat is underway. Be sure to praise their efforts as they learn new tasks. They will have more fun if they are involved. Show them where you are on the navigational chart and where you plan to go. Provide binoculars and point out interesting landmarks. If you're on a sailing yacht, explain how the sails work. Allow them to take the helm in calm weather, and be sure to take pictures of them having fun. If there are children in the group, crewmembers need to take turns keeping them amused with games, books, videos, and toys.

What happens to old crewmembers?

When you are fresh, young, and physically fit it's hard to imagine the day when you no longer want to work on yachts. The lifestyle is seductive, but things change and it's a fact that only a small percentage of professional crew carry on beyond their mid-40s.

With women, the reason is obvious since many of us leave the yachts to have children. Marriages between crewmembers have been known to continue happily for many years with the husband travelling while the missus stays home with the babies. A number of previously happy marriages also fail at this point. Dad can expect to miss all of his children's big moments. He will not be home for the first step, the first tooth, or the piano recital. And the long separations can eventually lead to infidelity. Sometimes unfounded jealousy creates an irrevocable rift in a relationship. The result is that many men also leave the industry when the babies come.

So what happens at the age of 42 when you really want to give up sailing. What are you going to do for a living? The logical move for many people is to get into the land-based side of the professional yachting industry. There are many businesses that cater to yachts. There are mechanics and riggers, surveyors, brokers, boatbuilders and training establishments. All of these are potential employers. There is currently a trend towards large multinational corporations forming within the yachting industry and they often employ former professional crew. (United Kingdom Sailing Academy, www.uksa.org, offers some interesting training for shore-based careers within the yachting industry.)

If you have an education in another field you might consider starting a new career in that area. Or you may try to develop a creative talent like writing, painting, or photography. These are popular choices because you can start them as hobbies while still working on the yachts.

Finally, retiring crewmembers if they were prudent generally have healthy savings put aside. With careful planning, they may be quite successful in starting up their own entrepreneurial ventures. The key is to work out what sort of business you want to start up and create your business plan before you actually retire from yachting.

GLOSSARY OF YACHTING TERMS

Sailing and power boating incorporate a language all their own. Here is a partial glossary of terms used aboard boats.

abaft	Toward the rear or stern of the boat.
abeam	At right angles to the keel of the boat, but not on the boat.
aboard	On or within the boat.
above deck	On the deck (not over it – see aloft).
abreast	Side by side; by the side of.
adrift	Loose, not on moorings or towline.
aft	Towards the stern of the boat.
aground	Touching or fast to the bottom.
ahead	In a forward direction.
aids to navigation	Artificial objects to supplement natural landmarks indicating safe and unsafe waters.
alee	Away from the direction of the wind; opposite of windward.
aloft	Above the deck of the boat.
amidships	In or toward the centre of the boat.

Familiarity with the terminology helps new crew acclimatise rapidly.

anchor roller	A roller over which the anchor chain is passed when at anchor.
anchorage	A place suitable for anchoring in relation to the wind, seas and bottom.
astern	In the back of the boat, opposite of ahead.
athwart ships	At right angles to the centreline of the boat; rowboat seats are generally athwart ships.
backstay	A wire support for the mast, usually running from the stern to the head of the mast.
batten	A flat piece of wood or fibreglass fitted into a pocket on the mainsail to stiffen the leech.
batten down	To secure hatches and loose objects both within the hull and on deck.
batten pocket	A pocket in the sail to hold the batten.
beam	The greatest width of the boat.

bear away	To alter course away from the direction of the wind.
bearing	The direction of an object expressed either as a true bearing as shown on the chart, or as a bearing relative to the heading of the boat.
belay	To make fast to a cleat or bollard.
below	Beneath the deck.
bight	The part of the rope or line, between the end and the standing part, on which a knot is formed.
bilge	A rounding of the hull along the length of the boat where the bottom meets the side.
binnacle	A support for the compass, raising it to a convenient position.
block	A pulley made of wood, metal or other material.
boat hook	A short shaft with a fitting at one end shaped to facilitate use in putting a line over a piling; recovering an object dropped overboard, or in pushing or fending off.
bobstay	Wire stay underneath the bowsprit; helps to counteract the upward pull exerted by the forestay.
boom	A spar that supports the foot of the sail.
boom vang	A block-and-tackle or hydraulic ram that controls the angle of the boom. Lowering the boom tightens the leech of the mainsail.
boot top	A painted stripe that indicates the waterline.
bow	The forward part of a boat.
bow line	A docking line leading from the bow.
bowline	Knot used to form a temporary loop in a line.

bowsprit	A short spar extending forward from the bow. Normally used to anchor the forestay.
bridge	The location from which a vessel is steered and its speed controlled.
bright work	Varnished woodwork and/or polished metal.
bulkhead	An interior partition commonly used to stiffen the hull. May be watertight.
bulls eye	A round eye through which a line is led, usually in order to change the direction of pull.
bulwark	A vertical extension above deck level designed to keep water out and sailors in the boat.
bunk	Sleeping berth.
buoy	An anchored float used for marking a position on the water, or a hazard, or a shoal; also used for mooring.
cabin	A compartment for passengers or crew.
capsize	To turn over.
capstan	Drum-like part of the windlass used for winding in rope, cables, or chain connected to cargo or anchors.
cast off	To let go.
catamaran	A twin-hulled boat, with hulls side by side.
centreboard	A board lowered through a slot in the centreline of the hull to reduce sideways skidding or leeway. Unlike a dagger board, which lifts vertically, a centreboard pivots around a pin.
chafing gear	Tubing or cloth wrapping used to protect a line from chafing on a rough surface.

chain plate	The fitting used to attach stays to the hull.
chart	A map for use by navigators.
chock	A fitting through which anchor or mooring lines are led.
cleat	A fitting to which lines are made fast.
clew	For a triangular sail, the aft most corner. On a mainsail the outhaul is attached to the clew; on genoas, the sheets are attached to the clew.
close-hauled	Sailing as close to the wind as possible with the sheets hauled aft and all sails drawing.
close reaching	(Fine reaching) Sailing with the wind between close-hauled and reaching.
clove hitch	A knot for temporarily fastening a line to a spar or piling.
coach roof	The cabin roof, raised above the deck to provide headroom in the cabin.
coaming	A vertical extension above the deck to prevent water from entering the cockpit. May be broadened to provide a base for winches.
cockpit	An opening in the deck from which the boat is handled.
coil	To lay a line (or water hose) down in circular turns.
companionway	The main entrance to the cabin, usually including the steps down into the cabin.
course	The direction in which a boat is steered.
cunningham	A control that adjusts the position of the draft in a sail by changing the tension on a sail's luff. Named after its inventor Briggs Cunningham.
current	The horizontal movement of water.

dagger board A board dropped vertically through the hull to prevent leeway. May be completely removed for sailing downwind.

danger zone The area encompassed from dead ahead of your boat to just abaft your starboard beam. You must stand clear of any boat in the 'danger zone'.

davits Small cranes used to raise or lower small boats and light items from deck to water level.

dead reckoning Also 'ded' reckoning. Abbreviation of deduced reckoning. A method of estimating the position of a ship without astronomical observations by applying previously determined position, the course and the distance travelled.

deck A permanent covering over a compartment, hull or any part thereof.

dinghy A small open boat, often used as a tender for a larger craft.

displacement The weight of water displaced by a floating vessel, thus, a boat's weight.

displacement hull A type of hull that plows through the water, displacing a weight of water equal to its own weight, even when more power is added.

ditty bag Small bag used for carrying and stowing small personal items or kits.

dock A protected water area in which vessels are moored. May denote a pier or a wharf.

dodger A screen, usually fabric, erected to protect the cockpit from spray and wind.

downhaul	A line used to pull a spar, such as the spinnaker pole, or a sail particularly the mainsail, down.
draft	The depth of water a boat draws.
ebb	A receding current.
fairlead	A fitting through which a rope or chain is led, to give a fair lead to a winch, cleat, sail, or anchor, or to prevent chafing.
fathom	Six feet.
fender	A cushion placed between boats, or between a boat and a pier, to prevent damage.
fid	A tool used by riggers to splice lines.
figure of eight knot	A knot in the form of a figure eight, placed in the end of a line to prevent the line from passing through a grommet or a block.
flood	An incoming current.
fluke	The palm of an anchor.
fo'c'sle	An abbreviation of forecastle. Refers to that portion of the cabin that is farthest forward. Often used as quarters for the crew.
following sea	An overtaking sea that comes from astern.
foot	The bottom edge of a sail.
fore and aft	In a line parallel to the keel.
foremast	Vertical spar most forward.
forepeak	The compartment farthest forward in the bow of the boat. Often used for anchor or sail stowage. May be the crew quarters in larger ships.
foresail	A sail set immediately before the mast.
forestay	Wire, sometimes rod, support for the mast running from the bowsprit or foredeck to a point at or near the top of the mast.

forward	Toward the bow of the boat.
fouled	Any piece of equipment that is jammed or entangled, or dirtied.
freeboard	The distance between the deck and the waterline. Most often it varies along the length of the boat.
furling	Stowing a sail on its boom by means of folding or flaking, and then lashing with sail ties. A foresail may also be rolled round a rotating stay.
GMDSS	Regulations on radio equipment for vessels over 300 gross tons. Requires Digitally Selective Communications (DSC) equipment. Smaller vessels also need certain equipment in order to communicate with the new distress frequencies.
gaff	A free swinging spar attached to the top edge of a sail.
galley	The kitchen area of a boat.
gangway	The area of a ship's side where people embark and disembark.
genoa	A large staysail.
give-way vessel	The vessel that must yield in meeting, crossing, or overtaking situations.
going about	The action of changing course when the wind is ahead, by steering the boat through the wind.
gooseneck	The mechanical joint that connects the boom to the mast.
goose wing	(Gull wing) To set the foresail and mainsail on opposite sides when running before the wind.
grab rails	Handhold fittings mounted on cabin tops and sides for personal safety when moving around the boat.
ground tackle	The anchor and its associated gear.

guardrail	A length of wire between the pulpit and pushpit, and running through or joined to the stanchions.
gunwale	The upper edge of the side of a boat.
guy	A line used to control the end of a spar. A spinnaker pole, for example, has one end attached to the mast, while the free end is moved back and forth with a guy.
gybe	Also jibe. To alter course with the wind astern, so that the stern goes through the wind and the boom passes from one side to the other.
halyard	A rope or wire attached to the head of a sail for hoisting and lowering.
hanks	Clips for securing a foresail to a stay.
hatch	An opening in the deck for entering below.
head	The top corner of a triangular sail. Also a marine toilet.
heading	The direction in which a vessel's bow points at any given time.
headsails	Any sail forward of the foremast.
headway	Forward motion of the boat opposite to sternway.
heave-to	A boat is hove-to when the foresail is backed (on the opposite side to the mainsail), as close to the wind as possible. The forward speed is very slow, but in rough weather any violent motion is much reduced.
helm	The wheel or tiller controlling the rudder.
helmsman	Sailor who steers the boat.
hiking stick	An extension of the tiller that enables the helmsman to sit at a distance from it.
hitch	A knot used to secure a rope to another object or to another rope, or to form a loop or a noose in a rope.

hold	A compartment below deck in a vessel, used solely for carrying cargo.
hull	The main body of a vessel.
IMO	The International Maritime Organisation. Creates and enforces the international shipping rules. As of July 2004, the IMO lists 164 member states. Each employs Port State Control inspectors to police these rules on all vessels.
ISM	Standards for safety management and operation of ships and for pollution prevention. Required by ships over 500 gross tons after July 2002, however several of the ISM requirements are a part of the MCA Code.
in irons	When the boat loses way, head to wind, and will not pay off on either tack.
inboard	More toward the centre of a vessel; inside; an engine fitted inside a boat.
inspection port	A watertight covering, usually small, that may be removed so the interior of the hull can be inspected or water removed.
jettison	To throw overboard.
jetty	A structure, usually masonry, projecting out from the shore; a jetty may protect a harbour entrance.
jib	A foresail set before the staysail.
jib lead	The block or fairlead, through which the jib sheet passes, between the clew of the jib and the winch.
jibe	See gybe.
keel	The principal structural member of the hull, which extends from the bow to the stern to which frames are attached. Also refers to a heavy length of metal

kicking strap
projecting below the bottom of the boat to aid stability and prevent movement of the boat sideways. (Boom vang) A rope and tackles that exert a downward pull on the boom to help adjust the shape of the mainsail.

knot (1)
A measure of speed equal to one nautical mile (6076 feet) per hour.

knot (2)
A fastening made by interweaving rope to form a stopper, to enclose or bind an object, to form a loop or a noose, to tie a small rope to an object, or to tie the ends of two small ropes together. A working knot should be easily tied as well as easily untied.

latitude
The distance north or south of the equator measured and expressed in degrees.

lazarette
A storage space in the boat's stern area.

lazy jack
Light lines from the topping lift to the boom, forming a cradle into which the mainsail may be lowered.

lead
Refers to the direction in which a line goes. A boom vang, for example, may 'lead to the cockpit'.

lee
The side sheltered from the wind.

lee helm
The tendency of a boat to bear off when the helm is released.

leech
The back edge of a sail.

leech line
A line running through the leech of the sail, used to tighten it.

leeward
The direction away from the wind. Opposite of windward.

leeway
The sideways movement of the boat caused by either wind or current.

lines
Rope or cordage used for various purposes aboard a boat.

log	A record of courses and operation. Also a device to measure speed.
longitude	The distance in degrees east or west of the prime meridian which passes through Greenwich, England.
loose-footed	A mainsail attached to the boom at the tack and clew, but not along the length of its foot.
luff	The forward edge of a sail. The flapping of a sail caused by the boat heading too close to the wind or because the sail is not trimmed tight enough.
luffing	Altering course toward the wind. In racing, luffing is a defence permitting a leeward boat to protect its wind from a boat passing to windward.
MCA	UK equivalent to the US Coastguard, but without military powers. They enforce the Merchant Shipping Act and have jurisdiction over any UK registered vessel.
mainmast	The tallest mast of the ship; on a schooner, the mast furthest aft.
mainsail	The sail set behind the main mast, the luff of which is supported by the mast.
Marpol	International Convention for the Prevention of Pollution from ships. Rules for discharging of oils and pollutants at sea, and the equipment and record keeping needed by vessels over 400 gross tons.
mast	A spar which supports the head and leading edge of the mainsail, and to which the foresails are hoisted.
mast step	Fitting or construction into which the base of the mast is placed.
midship	Equally distant from the bow and stern.

mizzen	A fore and aft sail flown from the mizzenmast.
mooring	An arrangement for securing a boat to a mooring buoy or a pier.
nautical mile	One minute of latitude; approximately 6076 feet – about 1/8 longer than the statute mile of 5280 feet.
navigation	The art and science of conducting a boat safely from one point to another.
navigation regulations	Also known as COLREGS. The regulations governing the movement of vessels in relation to each other, generally called steering and sailing rules.
oar	Device used to propel small boats by rowing.
outboard	Toward or beyond the boat's sides. A detachable engine mounted on a boat's stern.
outhaul	The control line that pulls the mainsail clew to the end of the boom, tightening the foot of the sail.
overboard	Over the side or out of the boat.
pay out	To feed line over the side of the boat, hand over hand.
pier	A loading platform extending at an angle from the shore.
pile	A wood or concrete pole driven into the bottom. May be used to support a pier.
pilot house	A small cabin on the deck of the ship that protects the steering wheel and the crewman steering.
pinch	To sail continually too close to the wind so that the sails are not properly filled and the boat loses way.

port	The left side of a boat looking forward; a harbour.
privileged vessel	A vessel which, according to the applicable navigation rule, has right-of-way.
pulpit	A metal framework on deck at the bow or stern. Provides a safety railing and serves as an attachment for the lifelines.
pushpit	Pulpit located on the stern.
quarter	The sides of a boat aft of midships.
quartering sea	Sea coming on the boats quarter.
rake	The masts inclination from vertical. Normally slightly aft.
reacher	A high-clewed genoa used when reaching in heavy winds.
reaching	Sailing with the wind on the beam.
reef points	A horizontal line of light lines on a sail, which may be tied to the boom, to reduce the area of the sail during heavy winds.
reefing	Reducing sail area.
riding turn	This occurs when the turns of the sheet around the winch drum become crossed and jam.
rigging	The lines that hold up the masts and move the sails.
roach	The area of a mainsail that extends beyond a straight line from the head to the clew. Battens usually support it.
rode	The anchor line and/or chain.
roller reefing	Reduces the area of a sail by rolling it around a stay, the mast, or the boom. Most common on headsails.
rope	In general, cordage as it is purchased at the store. When it comes aboard a vessel and is put to use it becomes a line.

rub-rail   Also rubbing strake. An applied or thickened member at the rail running the length of the boat; serves to protect the hull when alongside a pier or another boat.

rudder   A vertical plate or board for steering a boat.

run   To allow a line to feed freely.

running   Sailing with the wind aft.

running backstay   A stay that supports the mast from aft, usually from the quarter rather than the stern. When the boat is sailing downwind, the runner on the leeward side of the mainsail must be released so as not to interfere with the sail.

running lights   Lights required to be shown on boats underway between sundown and sun-up.

running rigging   The adjustable portion of the rigging, used to control sails and equipment.

SOLAS   International convention for Safety of Life at Sea. Standards for ship lifesaving, firefighting, communications and operation. These apply to vessels over 500 gross tons and to all passenger ships.

STCW   International convention for Standards of Training, Certification and Watchkeeping for seafarers. Standards for examination, courses at training schools, issuing of certificates, and operation of vessels.

sail   A piece of cloth that catches or directs the wind and so powers a vessel.

schooner   Sailing ships with at least 2 masts (foremast and mainmast) with the mainmast being the taller.

scope	The ratio of length of anchor rode in use to the vertical distance from the bow of the vessel to the bottom of the water. Usually six or seven to one for calm water; more in storm conditions.
screw	A boat's propeller.
scupper	Drain in cockpit, coaming, or toe-rail allowing water to drain out and overboard.
scuttle	A round window in the side or deck of a boat that may be opened to admit light and air, and closed tightly when required. May also refer to the intentional sinking of a ship.
sea cock	A through hull valve. A shut off on a plumbing or drainpipe between the vessel's interior and the sea.
sea room	A safe distance from the shore or other hazards.
secure	To make fast.
sheet	A rope attached to the clew of the sail by which the sail is trimmed as required; it is named after the sail to which it is attached, for example: genoa sheet.
sheet winch	A drum around which the sheets are turned to pull in and ease out the sails, may be geared to give mechanical advantage.
ship	A larger vessel usually thought of as being used for ocean travel. A vessel able to carry a 'boat' on board.
shroud	Wires that support the mast athwart ships.
skeg	A structural support to which the rudder is fastened on sailboats.

slack	Not fastened, loose. To loosen.
sounding	A measurement of the depth of water.
spar	A pole or beam.
spinnaker	A large balloon shaped sail hoisted forward of the forestay when reaching or running.
spreaders	Struts on the mast that brace the shrouds.
spring line	A pivot line used in docking, undocking, or to prevent the boat from moving forward or astern while made fast to the dock.
squall	A sudden, violent wind often accompanied by rain.
square knot	A knot used to join two lines of similar size. Also called a reef knot.
stanchions	Upright metal posts along the edge of the deck to which the guardrails are attached.
standing rigging	Permanent rigging used to support the spars. May be adjusted during racing, in some classes.
stand-on vessel	The vessel that has right-of-way in meeting, crossing, or overtaking situations.
starboard	The right side of a boat when looking forward.
stay	Wires that support the mast fore and aft eg 'forestay' and 'backstay'.
staysail	A triangular sail immediately forward of the mast, the luff of which is supported by the forestay.
stem	The foremost vertical part of the boat.
stern	The after part of the boat.
stern line	A docking line leading from the stern.
storm jib	A very small foresail for heavy weather.

storm trysail	A small strong sail set without a boom in heavy weather, in lieu of the mainsail.
stow	To put an item in its proper place.
swamp	To fill with water, but not settle to the bottom.
tack	The lower forward corner of a sail. Or turning the boat so that the bow passes through the eye of the wind. The side over which the main boom is carried defines the tack.
tacking	Making a course to windward by going about repeatedly, also known as 'beating'.
tackle	A mechanical device consisting of a rope rove through two or more blocks to increase the purchase of an applied pull.
taffrail	The rail at the stern of the boat.
telltales	Streamers attached to the sail to indicate wind flow.
thwart ships	At right angles to the centreline of the boat.
tide	The periodic rise and fall of water level in the oceans.
tiller	A bar or handle for turning a boat's rudder or an outboard motor.
toe-rail	A low rail, often slotted, along the side of the boat.
topping lift	A line or wire used to support the boom when the mainsail is not hoisted.
topsides	The sides of a vessel between the waterline and the deck.
to weather	A boat weathers an object by passing to windward of it. An object that is on the windward side of the boat is said to be up to weather.

trampoline	The fabric support between the hulls of a catamaran.
transom	The terminating structure of the hull at the stern of the boat.
trapeze	Wire gear enabling a crewmember to place all of his weight outboard of the hull, thus helping keep the boat level.
traveller	A fitting across the boat to which sheets are led. It can usually be adjusted from side to side so that the angle of the sheets can be changed.
trim	Fore and aft balance of a boat.
turnbuckle	(Bottle screw) A fitting for securing the stays or shrouds to the deck, consisting of a sleeve with a right-handed screw at one end and a left-handed screw at the other end.
underway	Vessel in motion, not secured to the land in any way.
vang	A device, usually with mechanical advantage, used to pull the boom down, flattening the sail.
veer	To let out rope or chain as when lowering the anchor. If applied to the wind, when the wind direction alters in a clockwise direction.
wake	Moving waves, track or path that a boat leaves behind it when moving across the waters.
waterline	A line painted on a hull which shows the point to which a boat sinks when it is properly trimmed.
weather helm	Also windward helm. The tendency of a boat to head up when the helm is released. Weather helm is measured in degrees of angle that the rudder must be turned to sail a straight course.

weighing anchor	To raise and secure the anchor.
winch	See sheet winch.
windward	The direction from which the wind is blowing.
yankee	A foresail flying above and forward of the jib, usually seen on bowsprit vessels.
yaw	To swing or steer off course, as when running with a quartering sea.
yawl	A small power boat used to provide steerage way when not under sail, or a sailboat rig with two masts, the aft one being shorter and located astern of the rudder post.

YACHT PARTS

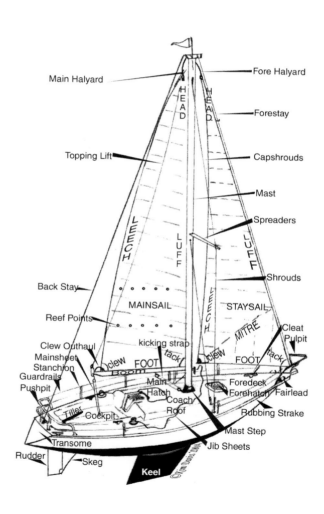

KNOTS AND LINE HANDLING

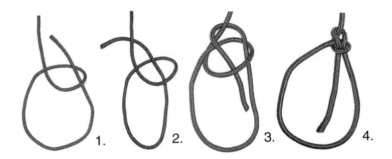

1.   2.   3.   4.

The bowline

The bowline is probably the most often used knot on a boat. This is because it will rarely slip before the breaking point of the line is reached. And just as important, it is easy to untie – even when wet.

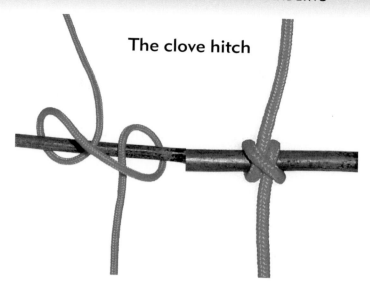

The clove hitch

This is a wonderful knot for tying fenders to the life lines on the yacht. You can tie it with a loop for quick release as well.

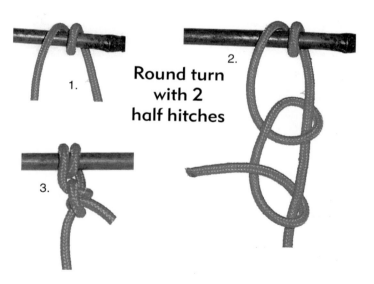

Round turn with 2 half hitches

1.

2.

3.

This knot is great for tying the dinghy to the rings at the dock.

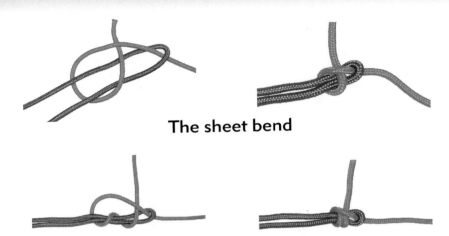

The sheet bend

The double sheet bend

These knots are used to join two lines of unequal thickness together.

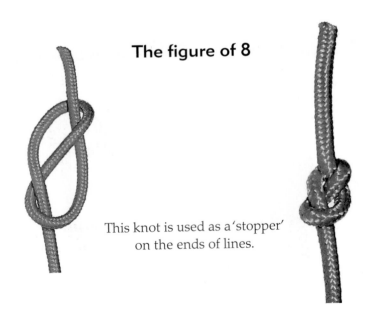

The figure of 8

This knot is used as a 'stopper' on the ends of lines.

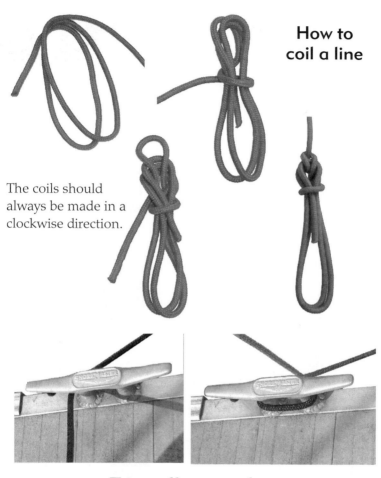

How to coil a line

The coils should always be made in a clockwise direction.

Tying off onto a cleat

Safe winch handling

Images 1, 2, and 3 above show the safe way to take in slack on a sheet using a winch. Winches always operate in a clockwise direction, so make your wraps around the winch go that way starting at the bottom of the winch (1) and wrapping 3 times around the winch (2) as you work toward the top of the winch and the jammer (3). To release tension from a sheet, first place your left hand on the coils around the winch, then release the sheet from the jammer (4). Gradually let the sheet out in a controlled fashion while keeping your left hand on the coils. Uncontrolled releasing of sheets can cause serious injury to everyone on deck, including the person releasing the sheet.

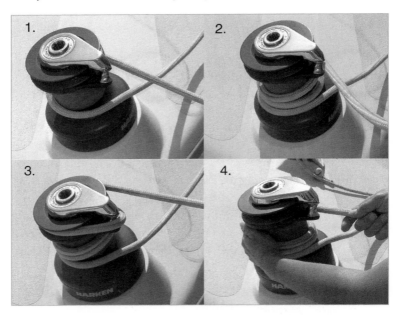

YACHT CREW PLACEMENT AGENCIES

This is a comprehensive worldwide listing of crew placement agencies, brokers who do crew placement, schools that offer crew placement and online services for people seeking crew positions. Wherever possible, have a look at the website first. Many of the agencies now insist that you submit your CV, fill out an online application, and make a credit card payment before they will even talk to you. At the end of this chapter there are some very good online services listed that are less expensive than the bricks and mortar variety of crew placement agencies. They operate online only and in general they are much younger than their traditional counterparts, so while you spend less money to register with them, there is also less certainty about landing a job with them.

A good relationship with a placement agency
will insure you get the 'top' jobs.

Asia & the South Pacific

Crew Asia Inc (A member of The Crew Network)

Suite 407 Cebu Holdings,
Cebu Business Park
6000 Cebu City
Philippines
Tel: +63 32 232 1732/ 231 0654
Mobile: +63 0 9173212230
Fax: +63 32 232 5180
Email: crewasia@pacific.net.ph
Web: www.crewasia.ph

Seal Super Yachts

225 Rat-U-Thit
200 Year Road
Patong Beach
Phuket 83150
Thailand
Tel: +(66) 76 340406 or
    +(66) 76 340932
Fax: +(66) 76 292242
Web: www.seal
    superyachts.com

Yacht Solutions Co Ltd

Phuket Boat Lagoon
20/27 Moo 2
Thepkrasattri Rd.
Koh Kaew
Muang, Phuket 83299
Thailand
Tel: +(66) 76 239114
Fax: +(66) 76 239139
Email: info@yachtsolutions.net
Web: www.yachtsolutions.net

Australia
Crew Pacific

Joy Weston – Owner/Operator
PO Box 25
Machans Beach
Cairns,
Australia 4878
Tel/fax: +61 (0) 7 4037 0113
Mobile: +61 (0) 407 789 527
Email: info@crewpacific.com.au
Web: www.crewpacific.com.au

Eastsail Pty Ltd

D'Albora Marinas
New Beach Road
Rushcutters Bay 2011
NSW Australia
Tel: + 61 (0) 2 9327 1166
Fax: +61 (0) 2 9328 1118
Email: jane@eastsail.com.au
Web: www.eastsail.com.au

Flying Fish

PO Box 155
Manly
2095 NSW
Australia
Tel: +61(0) 2 9976 6714
Fax: +61(0) 2 9976 6715
Email:
    flyingfish.online@bigpond.com
Web: www.flyingfishonline.com

Palm Beach Yachts International - Australia

Alan and Karen Birch
Tel: (561) 863 0082 or
    (0) 7 4773 9157
Fax: 561 863 4406
Email: birch@m141.aone.net.au
Web: www.yachtcrew.com

Yacht Crew Australia

Sanctuary Cove Marina
PO Box 428
Masthead Way
Queensland 4212
Australia
Tel: +61 (0) 7 55148222
Fax: +61 (0) 7 55148822
Email: info@
    yachtcrewaustralia.com
Web:
    http://yachtcrewaustralia.com

Canada

Illusion Marine Consultants

RR3, Bridgewater
NS B4V 2W2
Canada
Tel: (902) 543 3675
Fax: (902) 543 1718

Quadrant Marine Institute Inc

#14 - 2300 Canoe Cove Road
Sidney
BCV8L 3X9
Canada
Tel: +1 (250) 656 2824
Fax: +1 (250) 656 5092
Email:
    info@quadrantmarine.com
Web:
    www.quadrantmarine.com

Yacht Crew Register

Darcy Narraway
745 Tudor Avenue
North Vancouver
BCV7R1X1
Canada
Tel: +1 (604) 990 9901
    (Pacific time, GMT -9)
Email: info@yachtcrew.ca
Web: www.yachtcrew.ca

Caribbean

Caribbean Connections

Frances David
PO Box 3069
Road Town
Tortola
BVI
Tel: (800) 238 6912 or
    +1 (284) 494 3623
Fax: +1 (284) 494 4744
Email: caribcon@candwbvi.net

Flagship Inc

Carter Wilber
Yacht Haven Marina
5100 Long Bay Rd
St Thomas
USVI 00802
Tel: +1 (340) 774 5630
Fax: +1 (340) 776 3074
Email: carter@flagshipvi.com
Web: www.flagshipvi.com

The Maritime School of the West Indies

Located at:
Princess Resort & Marina
Port De Plaisance
Union Road 155
Cole Bay
St Maarten
Contact:
PO Box 822
Philipsburg
St Maarten
Netherland Antilles
Tel: +599 5 231209

Email: info@mswi.org
Web: www.mswi.org

The Moorings

Office is located on Tortola, but
correspondense goes through
the US head office.
19345 US 19 N #4
Clearwater
FL 33764-3147
USA
Tel: (888) 952 8420 or
   (727) 535 1446
Web: www.moorings.com

Croatia

Navicula

Eugena Kumicica 13/3
Rijeka
HR 51000
Croatia
Tel: +385 51 217 557 or
   +385 98 328 105
Fax: +385 51 216 147
Email: navicula@navicula.hr
Web: www.navicula.hr

France

Adrian J Fisher

Private Yacht Personnel Consultant
8 Avenue Mirambeau
06600 Antibes
France
Tel: +33 (0)4 9334 6547
Fax: +33 (0)4 9334 6523
Email: adrianfisher@riviera.fr

Blue Water Crew

La Galerie du Port
8 Blvd d'Aguillon
06600 Antibes
France
Tel : +33 (0) 4 93 34 34 13
Fax : +33 (0) 4 93 34 28 89
Email: crew@
   bluewateryachting.com

Camper & Nicholsons - Antibes

12 Avenue de la Liberation
06600 Antibes
France
Tel: +33 (0) 4 92 91 29 12
Fax: +33 (0) 4 92 91 29 00
Web:
   www.cnconnect.com/crew/

Claude Niek Yacht Broker

35 Route De Valbonne
06110 Le Cannet
France
Tel: +33 (0) 4 9318 0600
Fax: +33 (0) 4 9369 3698
Email: niek@imaninet.fr

The Crew Network

Corporate Headquarters
2bis, Avenue Thiers
06600 Antibes
France
Tel: +33 (0) 4 9721 1313
Fax: +33 (0) 4 9721 1314
Email: antibes@crewnetwork.com
Web: www.crewnetwork.com

Freedom Yachting

7 Blvd D'Aguillon
06600 Antibes
France
Tel: +33 (0) 4 9334 4773
Fax: +33 (0) 4 9334 7774
Email:
info@freedomyachting.com or
crew@freedomyachting.com
Web:
www.freedomyachting.com

International Crew Recruitment

16B Rue du 24 Aout
Antibes
France
Tel: +33 (0) 4 93 34 27 71
Mobile: +33 (0) 6 07 25 48 31
Fax: +33 (0) 4 93 34 27 93
Email: Stephen@intl-
crewrecruitment.com
Web: www.intl-
crewrecruitment.com

Peter Insull's Yacht Marketing - The Crew Agency

La Galerie du Port
8 Boulevard d'Aguillon
06600 Antibes
France
Tel: +33 (0) 4 93 34 6464
Fax: +33 (0) 4 93 34 2122
Email: crew@insull.com
Web:
www.insull.com/crew.html

Riviera Yacht Charter Inc

Contact: Raymond
Mobile: +33 (0) 663 373 747
Email:
charter@rivierayacht.com
Web: http://rivierayacht.com/
crew.htm

Sea Independence sarl - France

13, Avenue du 11 Novembre
06600 Antibes
France
Tel: +33 (0) 4 9334 5120
Fax: +33 (0) 4 9334 7159
Email: antibes@sea-
independence.com
Web: http://www.sea-
independence.com

Yacht Brokers International

Contact Jim Bradley about
Guardianage work
21 Rue Aubernon
06600 Antibes
France
Tel: +33 (0) 4 9334 0475
Mobile: +33 (0) 6 7597 4151
Email: jim@yachtbrokers
int.com
Web: www.yachtbrokers
int.com

YPI Crew

Les Residences du Port Vauban
17, Avenue du 11 Novembre
06600 Antibes
France
Tel: +33 (0) 4 92 90 46 10
Fax: +33 (0) 4 93 34 47 08
Email: info@ypicrew.com
Web: www.ypicrew.com

Germany
Crew Agency Germany

PO Box 1201
59512 Welver
Germany
Tel: +49 2384911127
Email: info@crewagency.de
Web: www.crewagency.de

Sea Independence SL - Germany

Steinstrasse 30
D-40210 Dusseldorf
Germany
Tel: +49 211 35 55 444
Fax: +49 211 35 55 499
Email: charter@sea-independence.com
Web: www.sea-independence.com

Weber & Odenwald –Yacht Affairs

Matthias Weber & Jendrik
Odenwald GbR
Vilser Schulstrasse 1a
D-27305 Bruchhausen-Vilsen
Germany
Tel: +49 (0) 171 6457508
Fax: +49 (0) 89 1488 291452
Email: info@yacht-affairs.com
Web: www.yacht-affairs.com

Monaco
Ocean Crew Member

30 Quai Jean-Charles Rey
98000 MC
Monaco
Fax: +377.97.77.81.11
Web:
www.oceancrewmember.com

New Zealand
The Crew Network

Thirty Seven South Ltd
15 Halsey Street
Westhaven
Auckland
New Zealand
Tel: +64 (0) 9 302.0178
Fax: +64 (0) 9 307 0871
Email: newzealand@
crewnetwork.com
Web: www.crewnetwork.com

Crewseeker South Pacific

6 Scorsby Street
Opua
New Zealand
Tel: +64 (0) 2 595 7977 or
+64 (0) 9 402 6070
Email: hepburn@island
cruising.co.nz
Web: www.islandcruising.co.nz

Nautilus Marine Ltd

PO Box 201
Westpark Village
West Harbour
1250 Auckland
New Zealand
Tel: +64 (0) 9 416 8113
Fax: +64 (0) 9 416 9113
Email:
info@nautilusmarine.co.nz
Web:
www.nautilusmarine.co.nz

Tallship Soren Larsen

Sail Training and Crew Positions
PO Box 310
Kumeu
1250 Auckland
New Zealand
Tel: +64 (0) 9 411 8755
Fax: +64 (0) 9 411 8484
Email:
escape@sorenlarsen.co.nz
Web: www.sorenlarsen.co.nz

Spain

Camper & Nicholsons – Palma

Club de Mar
07015 Palma de Mallorca
Spain
Tel: +34 971 40 33 11
Fax: +34 971 40 14 12
Web:
www.cnconnect.com/crew/

Crew Network - Yacht Help!

c/o Joan de Saridakis
Edificio Goya
1-A Marivent
07015 Palma de Mallorca
Spain
Tel: +34 971 402 878
Fax: +34 971 404 877
Email:
palma@crewnetwork.com
Web: www.crewnetwork.com

Fred Dovaston Crew

Miguel de Cervantes 23
Puerto Portals
07181 Mallorca
Spain
Tel: +34 971 677 375
Fax: +34 971 677 785
Email: fred@dovaston.com
Web: www.dovaston.com

Leticia Van Allen, SA

San Magin 36
07013 Palma de Mallorca
Spain
Tel: +34 670 532 773
Fax: +34 971 910 472
Email: info@leticiayachtcrew.com
Web: www.leticiayachtcrew.com

Sea Independence SL – Spain

Club de Mar
E-07015 Palma de Mallorca
Spain
Tel: +34 971 404 412

Fax: +34 971 402 327
Email: brokerage@sea-
  independence.com
Web: www.sea-
  independence.com

Yacht Engineers

Contact: George Parkinson
Calle Cotoner 58
07013 Palma de Mallorca
Spain
Tel: +34 971 28 18 13
Fax: +34 971 28 46 31
Email: info@yachtengineers.net
Web: www.yachtengineers.net

UK

Atlantic Marine / Maritime Atlantic Ltd

Maritime House
Basin Road North
Hove
Sussex
BN41 1WR UK
Tel: +44 (0) 1273 248800
Fax: +44 (0) 1273 248700
Email: info@atlantic-
  marine.co.uk
Web: www.atlantic-
  marine.co.uk

Auto Dynamic Positioning Services (ADPS)

Mayflower House
Armada Way
Plymouth
PL1 1LD UK

Tel: +44 (0) 1752 226797
Fax: +44 (0) 1752 268789
Web: www.adpsltd.com
Email: info@adpsltd.com

Crewseekers International

Hawthorn House
Hawthorn Lane
Sarisbury Green
Southampton
Hampshire
SO31 7BD
UK
Tel/fax: +44 (0) 1489 578319
Email: info@crewseekers.co.uk
Web: www.crewseekers.co.uk

Flying Fish

25 Union Road
Cowes
Isle of Wight
PO31 7TW
UK
Tel: +44 (0) 1983 280641
Tel UK: 0871 250 2500
Tel Australia: +61 (0) 2 9976
  6714
Fax: +44 (0) 1983 281821
Web: www.flyingfishonline.com

Global Crew Network

Attn: John Scott
145 Bracklyn Court
London
N1 7EJ
UK
Tel: +44 (0) 7773 361959

Fax: +44 (0) 207 253 4287

Email: info@globalcrew
network.com

Web:
www.globalcrewnetwork.com

Interior Crew

7 Riverview
Whippingham
Isle of Wight
PO32 6LU
UK
Tel: +44 (0) 1983 200 279
Email:
interiorcrew@freenet.co.uk

International Yacht Sales & Management Group

UK Office
Berry Head Farm
Brixham
TQ5 9AL
UK
Tel: +44 (0) 1803 850 050
Fax: +44 (0) 1803 851 011
Email: info@boats4ever.com
Web: www.boats4ever.com

United Kingdom Sailing Academy

West Cowes
Isle of Wight
PO31 7PQ UK
Tel: +44 (0) 1983 294941
Fax: +44 (0) 1983 295938
Email: info@uksa.org
Web: www.uksa.org

Viking Recruitment Limited

Aycliffe Business Centre
Archcliffe Road
Dover
Kent
CT17 9EL
UK
Tel: +44 (0) 1304 240881
Fax: +44 (0) 1304 240882
Email:
info@vikingrecruitment.com
Web:
www.vikingrecruitment.com

USA

Ancient Mariners

Captain Robert (Bob) Young
33 Branch Street
Scituate
MA 02066
USA
Tel: +1 (781) 545 4905
Email: cdrusnret@attbi.com
Web:
www.ancientmariners.com

Camper & Nicholsons – Ft Lauderdale

801 Seabreeze Blvd
Ft Lauderdale
FL 33316
USA
Tel: +1 (954) 524 4250
Fax: +1 (954) 524 4249
Web:
www.cnconnect.com/crew/

Captainsforhire.com

Captain John Jenkins
PO Box 1095
Westbrook
ME 04092
USA
Fax: (801) 838-5981
Email: CaptainJ@main.rr.com
Web: www.captainsforhire.com

Carole Manto Inc

412 SE 17th Street
Ft Lauderdale
FL 33316, USA
Tel: +1 (954) 523 2500
Fax: +1 (954) 523 2507
Email: info@carolemanto.com
Web: www.carolemanto.com

Coast to Coast Services Inc

2628-B Executive Place
PO Box 4414
Biloxi
MS 39535
USA
Tel: +1 (288) 388 5077
Fax: +1 (288) 388 6203
Email: info@c2cmarinejobs.com
Web: www.c2cmarinejobs.com

The Crew Network

1800 SE 10th Avenue
Suite 404
Ft Lauderdale
FL 33316
USA
Tel: +1 (954) 467 9777

Fax: +1 (954) 527 4083
Email: fortlauderdale@
     crewnetwork.com
Web: www.crewnetwork.com

Crew Unlimited

2067 South Federal Hwy
Ft Lauderdale
FL 33316
USA
Tel: +1 (954) 462 4624
Fax: +1 (954) 523 6712
Email: info@crewunlimited.com
Web: www.crewunlimited.com

Crew Unlimited - Newport

4 Broadway
Newport
Rhode Island 02840
USA
Tel: +1 401 847 8110
Fax: +1 401 848 0773
Email: newport@
     crewunlimited.com

Crewfinders International – Headquarters

404 & 408 SE 17th Street
Ft Lauderdale
FL 33316
USA
Tel: (800) 438 2739 or
     +1 (954) 522 2739
Fax: +1 (954) 522 2725
Email: crew@crewfinders.com
Web: www.crewfinders.com

Crewfinders International – Newport

2 Dean Avenue
Suite 5
Newport
RI 02840
USA
Tel: (866) 230 2739 or
 +1 (401) 849 5227
Fax: +1 (401) 849 5923
Email: crew@crewfinders.com
Web: www.crewfinders.com

D R Woods International

Ft Lauderdale
FL 33316
USA
Tel: +1 (954) 382 6125 or +1
(954) 524 0065
Email: info@drwyachting.com
Web: www.crewbydrwoods.com

Elite Crew International Inc

714 SE 17th Street
Ft Lauderdale
FL 33316
USA
Tel: +1 (954) 522 4840
Fax: +1 (954) 522 4930
Email: placement@elite
 crewintl.com
Web: www.elitecrewintl.com

Hinkley Crewed Charters

PO Box Six
15 Mansell Lane
Southwest Harbor
Maine 04679
USA
Tel: +1 (207) 244 0122 or
 (800) 504 2305
Fax: +1 (207) 244 0156
Email: Tina Hinckley
 tina@hinckleyyacht.com or
 Liz Harris cruise@
 hinckleyyacht.com
Web: www.hinckleyyacht.com

LaCasse Maritime Crew Service – Seattle

PO Box 189
Hansville
WA 98340
USA
Tel: +1 (206) 632 6858,
 +1 (360) 297 6630
Fax: +1 (360) 638 2079,
 +1 (360) 297 6631
Email:
 info@lacasseservices.com
Web: www.lacasseservices.com

LaCasse Maritime Crew Service – San Diego

1551 Shelter Island Dr
San Diego
CA 92106
USA
Tel: +1 (619) 523 2318
Fax: +1 (619) 523 3231
Email:
info@lacasseservices.com
Web: www.lacasseservices.com

Luxury Yacht Group LLC
1362 SE 17th Street
Ft Lauderdale
FL 33316
USA
Tel: +1 (954) 525 9959
Fax: +1 (954) 525 9949
Email: SJ@luxyachts.com
Web: www.luxyachts.com

Marine Jobs Inc
800 Downtowner Blvd
Suite 111
Mobile
AL 36609
USA
Tel: +1 (251) 380 0765
Fax: +1 (251) 380 0571
Web: www.marinejobs1.com

Offshore Passage Opportunities
PO Box 2600
Halesite
New York 11743
USA
Tel: +1 (631) 423 4988
Fax: +1 (631) 423 9009
Web: www.sailopo.com

Palm Beach Yachts International
4200 Flagler Drive
West Palm Beach
FL 33407
USA
Tel: +1 (561) 863 0082
Fax: +1 (561) 863 4406
Email: donna@yachtcrew.com
Web: www.yachtcrew.com

RYC & JH Palm Beach
2716 South Dixie Highway
West Palm Beach
FI 33405
USA
Tel: +1 (561) 366 8666
Fax: +1 (561) 366 8606
E-mail : palmbeach@
    rivierayacht.com
Web: http://rivierayacht.com

Voyager Marine Inc
PMB 224
1323 SE 17th Street
Ft Lauderdale
FL 33316
USA
Tel/fax: +1 (954) 974 7661
Mobile: +1 (954) 290 5187
Email: info@voyagermarine.org
Web: http://voyagermarine.org

Yachtcrews.com
757 SE 17th Street
PMB 703
Ft Lauderdale
FL 33316
USA
Tel: +1 (954) 540 4872
Email: info@yachtcrews.com
Web: www.yachtcrews.com

Yacht Delivery

San Diego, CA
Tel: (877) 807 6180 or
  +1 (619) 223 2537
Fax: +1 (619) 743 2336
Email: yachtdelivery@cox.net
Web: www.yachtdelivery.
  netfirms.com

Online Placement Services

Boating OZ Charters and Events

PO Box 358 Harbord
Sydney
2096 NSW
Australia
Tel: +61 (0408) 650 851
Email:
  boating@boatingoz.com.au
Web: www.boatingoz.com.au

Crewfile

Web: www.crewfile.com

Dockwalk

Web: www.dockwalk.com

International Seafarers Exchange

Web: www.jobxchange.com

International Yacht Restoration School – Job Opportunities

Web:
  www.iyrs.org/alumni/jobs.htm

JF Recruiting

Web: www.jf-recruiting.com

Jobs at Sea

Web: www.jobs-at-sea.com

Jobs on Yachts.com

Web: www.jobsonyachts.com

just4engineers - Joe Hodgson

Mobile: +44 (0)7713 635381
Email: joe@wizzwazz.com
Web: www.just4engineers.com

MUST Yacht and Ship Brokers

Marine Unlimited Services
Team
St. Martin – Caribbean
Web: www.sailingpoint.com
  /cc.shtml

ProCrew

Email: info@procrew.com
Web: www.procrew.com

Riviera Radio

Web: www.rivieraradio.mc/
  crewreview.html

Sailinglinks

Email: webcaptain@
  sailinglinks.com
Web: www.sailinglinks.com

Sailing San Francisco – Crew List + Bay Area Resources

Web: www.sfsailing.com

Waypoint 1

Web: www.wp1.co.nz

Yachtmama

Web: www.yachtmama.com

Yacht-Services.com

Email: admin@yacht-services.com

Web: www.yacht-services.com

YACHTCREW-CV.COM – Superyacht Services

Email: oceancrew@btopenworld.com

Web: www.yachtcrew-cv.com

Yacht Jobs – Make the Connection

Email: services@yachtie.net

Web: www.yachtie.net

APPENDIX

CREW AND SEAMANSHIP
TRAINING FACILITIES

The following list includes sail training and seamanship licensing organisations and schools that teach the specific skills professional crewmembers need. Where possible, check the websites first. This is only a partial list, so if you don't find a school in your area, try www.rya.org.uk. There you will find a search tool that will help you find an RYA certified training facility near you, wherever you might be in the world. In addition www.yachtmaster.com lists licensed training facilities worldwide.

Australia

Academy of Sail

PO Box 6065
Linden Park
Southern Australia 5065
Australia
Tel: +61 (0) 8 8338 4222
Fax: +61 (0) 8 8338 5566
Email: ac-sail@box.net.com
Web: www.academysail.com.au

Advance Sailing School

John F Keelty
116/21 East Crescent Street
McMahons Point
2060 NSW
Australia
Tel: +61 (0) 2 9955 5573 or
+61 (0) 4 2723 1682
Fax: +61 (0) 2 9956 7594
Email:
johnkeelty@bigpond.com
Web: www.users.bigpond.com/
johnkeelty

Allsail Yachting School

Graham Friend
On the Ferry Warf
McCarrs Creek Road
Church Point
2105 NSW
Australia
Tel: +61 (0) 2 9979 6266
Email: graham@allsail.com.au
Web: www.allsail.com.au

Australian Maritime College

PO Box 21
Beaconsfield 7270
Tasmania
Australia
Tel: +61 (0) 3 6335 4442 or
+61 (0) 3 6335 4711
Mobile: +61 419 777 680
Email: d.breckenridge@
fme.amc.edu.au
Web: www.amc.edu.au

Bayside Marine Training Center

Marshall H Miller
Location: Shop 1
108-112 Florence Street
Wynnum
Queensland 4178
Australia
Postal Address: PO Box 5392
Manly
Queensland 4179
Australia
Tel: +61(0)7.3396.0689
Email: marshall@
powerandsailtraining.biz
Web: www.
powerandsailtraining.biz

Bramble Bay Sailing School

29 Swan Street
Shorncliffe
Brisbane
Queensland 4017
Australia

Tel: +61 (0) 7 3869 0248

Email:

bramble_bay@hotmail.com.au

Crew Pacific

Joy Weston – Owner/Operator

PO Box 25

Machans Beach

Cairns 4878

Australia

Tel/fax: +61 (0) 7 4037 0113

Mobile: +61 (0) 407 789 527

Email: info@crewpacific.com.au

Web: www.crewpacific.com.au

Eastsail Pty Ltd.

D'Albora Marinas

New Beach Road

Rushcutters Bay 2011

NSW

Australia

Tel: + 61 (0) 2 9327 1166

Fax: +61 (0) 2 9328 1118

Email: jane@eastsail.com.au

Web: www.eastsail.com.au

Flying Fish

PO Box 155

Manly

2095 NSW

Australia

Tel: +61 (0) 2 9976 6714

Fax: +61 (0) 2 9976 6715

Email:

flyingfish.online@bigpond.com

Web: www.flyingfishonline.com

Freemantle Sailing Club

PO Box 860

Freemantle

6959 WA

Australia

Tel: +61 (0) 8 9335 8800

Fax: +61 (0) 8 9430 5396

Email: admin@fsc.com.au

Web: www.fsc.com.au

Funsail

Barry Barnes

145 Ocean Vista Drive

Maroochy River

Queensland 4561

Australia

Tel: +61 (0) 7 5446 6410

Mobile: +61 (0) 418 243 042

Fax: +61 (0) 7 5446 6203

Email: barryb@funsail.com.au

Web: www.funsail.com.au

Getaway Sailing Adventures

Shop 64 B

Quay Side

Roseby Street

Birkenhead Point

Drummoyne

2047 NSW

Australia

Tel: +61 (0) 2 9181 1911

Mobile: +61 (0) 411 339 000

Fax: +61 (0) 2 9181 1636

Email: information@

getaway-sailing.com

Web: www.getaway-sailing.com

Sail training vessels teach sailing and teamwork.

Gullivers Sail Training School

Grant (Skip) Batkin
41 Trevellyan Street
Cronulla
2230 NSW
Australia
Tel: +61 (0) 2 9523 6872
    or +61 (0) 401 615 800
Email: skip@sailtraining.com.au
Web: www.sailtraining.com.au

Learn to Sail By Mail

PO Box 312
Swansea, NSW 2281
Australia
Mobile: +61 (0) 409 149 159
Fax: +61 (0) 2 4971 0099
Email: jim.orrell@bigpond.com

Web:
    www.learntosailbymail.com

Melbourne Sailing School

46 Balmoral Drive
Parkdale
3195 VIC
Australia
Tel/fax: +61(0) 3 9587 8517
Email:
    sailing@melbsailing.com.au
Web: www.melbsailing.com.au

OYM Training

Location:
Western Port Marina
Mullet St
Hastings
Australia

Postal Address:
PO Box 171
Hastings
Victoria 3915
Australia
Tel/fax: +61 (0) 3 5979 7353
Mobile: +61 (0) 418 399 687
Email: enquiries
@oymtraining.com.au
Web: www.oceanyachtmaster.
com.au

Pacific Sailing School

Location:
Cruising Yacht Club of Australia
New Beach Rd
Rushcutters Bay
NSW 2026
Sydney
Australia
Postal Address:
PO Box 249
Edgecliff, Sydney
2027 NSW
Australia
Tel: +61 (0) 2 9326 2399
Fax: +61 (0) 2 9327 2487
Email: info@pacific
sailingschool.com.au
Web: www.pacific
sailingschool.com.au

Queensland Yachting Association School

138 Quay Street
PO Box 19
Bulimba

4171 Queensland
Australia
Tel: +61 (0) 7 3399 1111
Fax: +61 (0) 7 3399 7700
Email:
office@qldyachting.org.au
Web: www.qldyachting.org.au

Sailing With Attitude

Jonathan Jean Bogais
Based at the Sydney Fish
Market Marina
Pyrmont
Sydney, Australia
Tel: +61 (0) 2 9500 0046
Mobile: +61 (0) 438 724 546
Email: jonathan@sailing
withattitude.com.au
Web: www.sailingwithattitude.
com.au

Simply Sailing

PO Box 344
Seaforth
NSW 2092
Australia
Tel: +61 (0) 2 9451 2511 or
+61 (0) 2 9969 6997
Mobile: +61(0) 418 444 842 or
+61 (0) 408 277 073
Fax: +61(0)2 9452 1415
Email:
info@simplysailing.com.au
Web:
www.simplysailing.com.au

South Pacific Sailing School

PO Box 339
Airlie Beach
4802 Queensland
Australia
Tel/fax: +61 (0) 7 4946 1300
Email: ahoy@sailtrain.com
Web: www.sailtrain.com

Southern Cross School of Yachting

170 Stratton Terrace
Manly
Queensland 4179
Australia
Tel: +61 (0) 7 3396 4100
Fax: +61 (0) 7 3396 9598
Email: sailing@southern
crossyachting.com.au
Web: www.southerncross
yachting.com.au

Sunshine Coast Sailing Academy

PO Box 5202
Maroochydore South
4558 Queensland
Australia
Tel/fax: +61 (0) 7 5478 2299
Email:
oceanman@learn2sail.com.au
Web: www.learn2sail.com.au

Wind Dancer Cruising

PO Box 153
Toronto
2283 NSW

Australia
Tel: +61 (0) 4 1844 2755
Fax: +61 (0) 2 4959 8894
Email: sea.g@bigpond.com
Web: www.winddancer.com.au

Yachtmaster Sailing School

266 Dorcas Street
South Melbourne
3205
Australia
Tel: +61 (0) 3 9699 9425
Fax: +61 (0) 3 9600 9208
Email:
yacht@yachtmaster.com.au
Web: www.yachtmaster.com.au

Yachtpro (St Kilda)

C/o Royal Melbourne Yacht
Squadron
PO Box 2000
Pier Road
St Kilda West
3182 Victoria
Australia
Tel: +61(0) 3 9525 5221
Email: sail@yachtpro.com.au
Web: http://yachtpro.com.au

Canada
Cooper Boating

1620 Duranleau Street
Granville Island
Vancouver
British Columbia
V6H 3S4
Canada

Tel: +1 (604) 687 4110 or
   (888) 999 6419
Fax: +1 (604) 687 3267
Web: www.cooperboating.com

Quadrant Marine Institute Inc

#14 - 2300 Canoe Cove Road
Sidney
British Columbia
V8L 3X9
Canada
Tel: +1 (250) 656 2824
Fax: +1 (250) 656 5092
Email: info@quadrantmarine.com
Web:
   www.quadrantmarine.com

Richmond Sailcraft Yacht Charters Ltd

10231 Ainsworth Crescent
Richmond
BC V7A-3V3
Canada
Tel: +1 (604) 277 2739 or
   (877) 277 2739
Email: info@sailcraft.com
Web: www.sailcraft.com

Captain's Yacht Training and Charters

Email: info@sailingcaptain.com
Web: www.sailingcaptain.com

Caribbean
The Maritime School of the West Indies

Located at:
Princess Resort & Marina
Port De Plaisance
Union Road 155
Cole Bay
St Maarten
Postal address:
PO Box 822
Philipsburg
St Maarten
Netherland Antilles
Tel: +599 5 231209
Email: info@mswi.org
Web: www.mswi.org

France
Blue Water Training

La Galerie du Port
8 Blvd D'Aguillon
06600 Antibes
France
Tel: +33 (0) 4 9334 3413
Fax: +33 (0) 4 9334 3593
Email: training@
   bluewateryachting.com
Web: www.
   bluewater-charter.com

Brittany Sail

Richard & Sue Curtis
L'Ancrage
Kergalet
Lanveoc
29160 Finistere

France
Tel: +33 (0) 2 9817 0131
Email: info@brittanysail.co.uk
Web: www.brittanysail.co.uk

Freedom Yachting

7 Boulevard d'Aguillon
06600 Antibes
France
Tel: +33 4 9334 4773
Fax: +33 4 9334 7774
Email: training@
    freedomyachting.com or
    info@freedomyachting.com
Web:
    www.freedomyachting.com

Ocean Pro - South of France

Tel: +33 (0) 4 9353 6595
Email: info@oceanpro.co.uk
Web: www.oceanpro.co.uk

New Zealand

Bay of Islands Sailing School Ltd

100 Riverview Road
Kerikeri
Bay of Islands
New Zealand
Tel: +64 9 407 1618
Email: Stuart.riddle@xtra.co.nz

Gulfwind Limited

PO Box 87-318
Meadowbank
Auckland
New Zealand
Tel: +64 (09) 521 1564
Mobile: +64 027 480 2462
Fax: +64 (09) 521 1567
Email: info@gulfwind.co.nz
Web: www.gulfwind.co.nz

Mahurangi Technical Institute

PO Box 414
11 Glenmore Drive
Warkworth
New Zealand
Tel: +64 (09) 425 8493
Freephone: 0800 DONT SINK
Fax: +64 (09) 425 8928
Email: info@mti.net.nz
Web: www.mahurangitech.co.nz

Sunsail South Pacific Sailing School

PO Box 33729
Takapuna
Auckland 1332
New Zealand
Tel: +64(09)378-7900
Email:
    info@sunpacificsailing.com
Web:
    www.sunpacificsailing.com

Tallship Soren Larsen

Sail Training and Crew Positions
PO Box 310
Kumeu
Auckland 1250
New Zealand
Tel: +64 (0) 9 411 8755

Fax: +64(0) 9 411 8484
Email:
  escape@sorenlarsen.co.nz
Web: www.sorenlarsen.co.nz

South Africa
Ocean Sailing Academy
327 West Quay Building
West Quay Road
Cape Town 8001
South Africa
Web: www.oceansailing.co.za
Durban:
Tel: +27 31 301 5726
Fax: +27 31 307 1257
Email:
  academy@oceansailing.co.za
Cape Town:
Tel: +27 21 425 7837
Fax: +27 21 421 8841
Email:
  oceansailing@telkomsa.net

Professional Yachtmaster Training in South Africa
10 Fenton Road
Durban
South Africa
Tel: +27 (0) 31 307 4992
Fax: +27 (0) 37 307 4999
Email: info@pyt.co.za
Web: www.pyt.co.za

Sunsail Maritime Academy
Web: www.sunsail.co.za
Durban:
Tel: +27 31 307 7944
Fax: +27 31 306 2066
Email:
  bonnet@yachtsman.co.za
Cape Town:
Tel: +27 21 465 8789
Fax: +27 21 465 1894
Email: sailinginfo@
  sunsailcapetown.co.za

Yachtmaster Ocean Services
PO Box 12181
Mill Street
8010 Cape Town
South Africa
Tel/fax: +27 21 462-3413
Email: skipper@yachtmaster.co.za

Spain
Balearic Sea School
Mallorca
Locales 55-56
Puerto Portals
07181
Calvia
Mallorca
Spain
Tel: +34 606 859 560
Fax: +34 971 000 000
Email:
  info@balearicseaschool.com
Web:
  www.balearicseaschool.com

Blue Water Training

Tel/fax: +34 971 677 154

Email: bluewateryachting
palma@telefonica.net

Web: www.bluewater-
charter.com

Hamble School of Yachting – Balearics

Paseo Maritimo 1

Puerto Alcudiamar

Local 5a

07410 Alcudia

Mallorca

Spain

Tel: +34 971 547 889

Fax: +34 971 897 34965

Email:
info@hamblebalearics.com

Web:
www.hamblebalearics.com

Hornblower Sea School

Carrer D'Elcano

07470 Puerto Pollenca

Mallorca

Spain

Tel: +34 971 549 955

Email:
info@hornblower.eu.com

Web: www.hornblower.eu.com

Mallorca Sea School

Local 37

E-07015

Puerto Portals

Mallorca

Spain

Tel: +34 971 679 342

Email: mallorcassc@terra.es

Web:
www.mallorcaseaschool.info

Saracen Sailing

Apartado 162

E-07460

Pollensa

Mallorca

Spain

Tel: (International) +44 (0) 845
330 1357 (Mallorca) +34 971
509 519

Email:
office@saracensailing.com

Web: www.saracensailing.com

Sea Teach SL

Port Petit 324

07660 Cala D'or

Mallorca

Spain

Tel/fax: +34 971 648 429

Mobile: +34 626 090 664 or
+34 626 275 264

Email: email@sea-teach.com

Web: www.sea-teach.com

Turkey
Portway Gocek (Turkey)

Göcek 48310

Fethiye

Turkey

Tel: +90 252 6452599

Fax: +90 252 6452326

Email:
charter@portwayturkey.com
Web: www.portwayturkey.com

Email:
seaschool@dartsailing.co.uk
Web: www.dartsailing.co.uk

UK
Auto Dynamic Positioning Services (ADPS)
Mayflower House
Armada Way
Plymouth PL1 1LD
UK
Tel: +44 (0) 1752 226797
Fax: +44 (0) 1752 268789
Email: info@adpsltd.com
Web: www.adpsltd.com

Bisham Abbey Sailing School
Bisham Abbey National Sports
Centre
Bisham
Near Marlow, Bucks
SL7 1RT
UK
Tel: +44 (0) 1628 474960
Web: www.bishamabbey
sailing.co.uk

Dart Sailing School
9 Smith Street
Dartmouth
Devon
TQ6 9QR
UK
Tel/Fax: +44 (0) 1803 833973
Mobile: +44 (0) 7970 893222
or 223

Flying Fish
25 Union Road
Cowes
Isle of Wight
PO31 7TW
UK
Tel: +44 (0) 1983 280641
Tel UK: 0871 250 2500
Tel Australia: 02 9976 6714
Fax: +44 (0) 1983 281821
Web: www.flyingfishonline.com

Hamble School of Yachting
Mercury Yacht Harbour
Satchell Lane
Hamble
Hampshire
SO31 4HQ
UK
Tel: +44 (0) 23 8045 2668
Fax: +44 (0) 23 8045 6687
Email: tuition@hamble.co.uk
Web: www.hamble.co.uk

Haslar Sea School
Haslar Marina
Haslar Road
Gosport
Hampshire
PO12 1NU
UK
Tel: +44 (0) 23 9252 0099
Fax: +44 (0) 23 9252 0100

Email:
  info@haslarseaschool.co.uk
Web:
  www.haslarseaschool.co.uk

Hobo Yachting

Jenny and Ken Campling
9A Carlton Road
Southampton
Hampshire
SO15 2HN
UK
Tel/fax: +44 (0) 23 8033 4574
Email:
  jenny@hoboyachting.co.uk
Web: www.hoboyachting.co.uk

Lighthouse Sailing School

100 Billacombe Road
Plymstock
Plymouth
PL9 7EZ
UK
Tel: +44 (0) 1752 481575
Email:
  info@lighthousesailing.co.uk
Web:
  www.lighthousesailing.co.uk

Plymouth Sailing School

Anne's Battery
Coxside
Plymouth
Devon
PL4 0LP
UK
Tel: +44 (0) 1752 667170

Fax: +44 (0) 1752 257162
Email:
  school@plymsail.demon.co.uk
Web: www.plymsail.co.uk

Tall Ships Youth Trust Limited

2A The Hard, Portsmouth
Hants, PO1 3PT
Tel: 02392 832055
Fax: 02392 815769
Email:
  reservations@tallships.org
Web: www.tallships.org

Southern Professional Training

305 Swanwick Lane
Swanwick
Southampton
Hampshire
SO31 7GT UK
Tel: +44 (0) 1489 575511
Fax: +44 (0) 1489 578828
Email: sailing@southern.co.uk
Web: www.southern.co.uk

United Kingdom Sailing Academy

West Cowes
Isle of Wight
PO31 7PQ
UK
Tel: +44 (0) 1983 294941
Fax: +44 (0) 1983 295938
Email: info@uksa.org
Web: www.uksa.org

Yachtmaster Training Ltd

Online training course
Tel: +44 (0) 23 8067 8723
Fax: +44 (0) 23 8055 0143
Email:
    enquiry@yachtmaster.co.uk
Web: www.yachtmaster-
    training.ltd.uk

USA
American Yacht Institute

1003 SE 17th St
Ft Lauderdale
FL 33316
USA
Tel: +1 (954) 522-1044
Fax: +1 (954) 522-0889
Email: info@american
    yachtinstitute.com
Web: www.american
    yachtinstitute.com

Chapman School of Seamanship

4343 SE St Lucie Blvd.
Stuart
FL 34997
USA
Tel: (800) 225 2841 or
    +1 (772) 283 8130
Fax: +1 (772) 283 2019
Email: info@chapman.org
Web: www.chapman.org

D R Woods International

Ft Lauderdale
FL 33316
USA
Tel: +1 (954) 382 6125 or
    +1 (954) 524 0065
Email: info@drwyachting.com
Web: www.crewbydrwoods.com

Fremont Maritime Services

1019 West Ewing Street
Seattle
WA 98119
USA
Tel: +1 (206) 782 4308
Email: info@freemont
    maritime.com
Web: www.sea-safety.com

International Yachtmaster Training Inc (various locations worldwide – see website)

910 SE 17th Street
Ft Lauderdale
FL 33316
USA
Tel: +1 (954) 779 7764
Fax: +1 (954) 779 7165
Email: info@yachtmaster.com
Web: www.yachtmaster.com

International Yacht Restoration School

449 Thames Street
Newport
RI 02840
USA
Tel: +1 (401) 848 5777
Fax: +1 (401) 842 0669
Email: info@iyrs.org
Web: www.iyrs.org

Maine Maritime Academy

Castine
ME 04420
USA
Tel: +1 (207) 326 2206
Email: admissions@mma.edu
Web: www.mainemaritime.edu
(see continuing education for STCW – 95 courses)

Maritime Professional Training

1915 South Andrews Avenue
Ft Lauderdale
FL 33316
USA
Tel: (888) 839 5025 or
+1 (954) 525 1014
Email: info@mptusa.com
Web: www.mptusa.com

Ocean Voyages Inc (Tall Ships)

1709 Bridgeway
Sausalito
CA 94965
USA
Tel: (800) 299 4444 or
+1 (415) 561 3435
Fax: +1 (415) 332 7460
Email: sail@oceanvoyages.com
Web: www.oceanvoyages.com

Sea School - Head Office

8440 4th Street North
St Petersburg
FL 33702
USA
Tel: (800) 237 8663 or +1 (727)
577 3992
Web: www.seaschool.com
(see website for numerous other locations)

STAR Center

2 West Dixie Highway
Dania Beach
FL 33004
USA
Tel: +1 (954) 921 7254 or
(800) 445 4522
Web: www.star-center.com

INDEX